**Controversies in Pol**

*Controversies in Contextual Theology Series*

# Controversies in Political Theology: Development or Liberation?

Thia Cooper

scm press

British Library Cataloguing in Publication data

A catalogue record for this book is available from the British Library

978 0 334 04112 2

First published in 2007 by SCM Press
13–17 Long Lane,
London EC1A 9PN

www.scm-canterburypress.co.uk

SCM Press is a division of
SCM-Canterbury Press Ltd

Typeset by Regent Typesetting, London
Printed and bound in Great Britain by
MPG Books Ltd, Bodmin, Cornwall

# Contents

To Cynthia and Marcella

# List of abbreviations

| | |
|---|---|
| BEC | base ecclesial community |
| CAFOD | Catholic Fund for Overseas Development |
| CCPD | Commission on the Churches' Participation in Development |
| CEAS | *Centro de Estudos e Ação Social* (Centre for Studies and Social Action) |
| CSO | civil society organization |
| DfID | Department for International Development |
| GRA | global regulating authority |
| IMF | International Monetary Fund |
| MST | Movimento dos Trabalhadores Ruraís sem Terra |
| NGO | non-governmental organization |
| SCAC | Scottish Christian Aid Committee |
| SODEPAX | Joint Committee on Society, Development and Peace |
| TNC | transnational corporation |
| WCC | World Council of Churches |
| WTO | World Trade Organization |

# Acknowledgements

Thanks to: Marcella Althaus-Reid and Lisa Isherwood for publishing this book in their series; Barbara Laing at SCM Press; staff and supporters of both Christian Aid and CEAS for their openness and kindness; in particular, the Churches and Scottish teams at Christian Aid and Rita Santa Rita at CEAS; the staff at *Albergue das Laranjeiras*; the former Faculty Group of Arts, Divinity and Music at the University of Edinburgh, the University of Edinburgh Development Trust, and Gustavus Adolphus College's Faculty Development Committee for their financial support; my writing group: Alisa and Katy and later Deborah; Esther; and finally my colleagues at Edinburgh and Gustavus.

## Note on inclusive language

While I have used inclusive language in my own writing, many older documents use 'man'/'men' etc., which was normally assumed to include women. I have left these quotations unchanged.

# Introduction

## Getting involved is part of the Christian witness: Fieldwork diary, Edinburgh, Scotland, 14 November 2002

I entered the church on George IV Bridge, soaked and cold from the short walk in the Edinburgh rain. I hung up my rain jacket and spent the next few minutes in the foyer drinking tea, and chatting with several committee members. Gradually we made our way into the sanctuary itself where chairs and tables were arranged in front of the altar in a square for the 30 of us. We were a mixture of men and women, all but two of us were white, and perhaps only three of us were under 40, although I never asked for ages! The morning session was given over to an interview with Daleep Mukarji, Christian Aid's[1] director. He is a tall Indian man, with short, dark brown hair and a booming voice, a medical doctor by training. He had circles under his eyes, suggesting a lack of sleep, but he strode back and forth as he talked, making eye contact with each person who asked a question and, in fact, with most of the participants in the room, at some point. He was the head of one of Christian Aid's partners in India for several years before moving on to

---

1 Christian Aid is a British and Irish faith-based aid and development organiza-tion, funding overseas partners to carry out relief, development work and advocacy, while it focuses on advocacy work itself in the North. It was set up after World War Two by the British Council of Churches, which later became Churches Together in Britain and Ireland, to provide aid to refugees in Europe and later expanded to organizations across the globe. It is now sponsored by 41 UK church denominations. See www.christian-aid.org.

a position with the World Council of Churches[2] and then the director-ship of Christian Aid.

One man with glasses and a ginger beard asked how Mukarji saw Christian Aid as distinctive from other UK aid agencies. Mukarji began by saying that its role as the churches' relief and development agency makes it unique. Christian Aid is owned by and rooted in the churches. They 'make it possible for us to do our work,' he said, and stated that he is proud of being inspired by the gospel in this way. Because of this foun-dation, Christian Aid takes the biblical, theological, and missiological dimensions of its work seriously. He said this does not mean that its goal is to make people Christian or to help only Christians. It is to act from a Christian basis because the gospel says that 'Christians are to share the love of Jesus', as 'all are made in God's image'.

As I looked around the table, I saw several of the committee members lean forward in response to his words, many of them nodding. He con-tinued by explaining that Christian Aid considers it a privilege to work with partners overseas. It identifies grassroots organizations to fund, which it hopes to 'be inspired by'.

He was next asked how Christian Aid maintained its focus on overseas partners, when less and less of its budget is directed toward them. He replied that partners still receive 75 per cent of the income of Christian Aid to do development and advocacy work in their own countries. In addition, up to 15 per cent is now spent on education, policy, and campaigning in the UK and internationally. He said that developing countries do not want aid, they want to be part of international trade, to be able to participate in the global trading system. That is one of the reasons for Christian Aid's campaign, 'Trade for Life'.[3]

Another participant asked whether Christian Aid supporters wanted their money to be spent on advocacy work like the campaign or whether

---

2 The World Council of Churches is an international ecumenical Christian organization established in 1948 to promote dialogue and action between the world's Christians. See www.wcc-coe.org for further details.

3 This campaign will be detailed in Chapter 5. It aimed to change the rules of international trade to prioritize the poor.

they just wanted their donation to be spent on aid. Mukarji answered that this is a challenge for an organization like Christian Aid. It has to accept churches and supporters where they are but continue to educate them. There are long-time supporters who have confidence in Christian Aid and understand that 'you can't handle the symptoms without looking at the root causes' of poverty. However, other supporters may not be aware of the larger issues, such as the fact that 'what you buy in the shops has an impact', as does 'how you invest your money'. This is where the worship and Bible study material should help to show the links to wider issues.

People can begin to engage with Christian Aid at the level of providing money for relief work and later move on to understanding development and, finally advocacy, Mukarji continued. It is a process. 'For Christians, getting involved in the concerns of this world is not political and the church has a huge heritage in this area.' Christians have been involved in prison reform, poverty eradication in the UK, and in the civil rights movements in America, for example. So why would it not be natural to look at poverty issues around the world inspired by faith? Every human being is created in God's image with needs and rights. Christian Aid is not apologetic for campaigning. There is a need to challenge people to 'stand up, speak out, take sides'. That is the prophetic role of the churches.

He ended by stating Christian Aid's constitutional mandate: to expose the scandal of poverty, to contribute to the eradication of poverty by the partners, and to challenge structures and systems to eradicate poverty too. 'Getting involved is part of the Christian witness.' There is no point in funding only development projects; international and economic systems also have to be influenced. Mukarji cited Clare Short (former UK Secretary of State for International Development), who once said that it is the middle classes who are trying to 'do good' in developing countries, but added that he thinks it is more than this. It is the 'faith-base' taking action.

Christian Aid is a faith-based civil society organization (CSO). This excerpt from my research diary has described part of a meeting within Christian Aid, an interview between its director and a group of people involved with Christian Aid in Scotland.[4] This group formed to ensure that the Christian churches in Scotland alongside Christian Aid deal with issues of faith and development. Christian Aid wants to integrate their Christianity and practice as they work toward development.

What is development? A common definition of development is 'economic growth with poverty reduction'. This definition is used by many aid agencies, governments, and policy makers, including Christian Aid. However, those living with the effects of development on the ground often have a different and negative definition, as I'll explore later in Chapter 1.

## Should Christians work toward development or liberation?

In 1987, Charles Elliott, former Christian Aid director, explained why this question is not so easy to answer, even though he and his colleagues faced the question on a daily basis:

> The theological work undertaken by the development agencies is most noticeable for its absence or low quality. For the development activists regarded theology as irrelevant. The tragedy is that, given the kind of theology that was being written and debated in most metro-politan countries, they were quite right. It had to wait for various strands of thought that are usually lumped under the umbrella of liberation theology to appear, significantly, from the developing world itself before theology had anything significant to say concerning what was going on. (Elliott, 1987, p. 45)

It is this situation and context that I explore in this book. The Christian basis for development is not clear. There is not a prominent theology of development in the same way that the theology of liberation emerged from Latin America in the 1960s and 70s. Yet, themes emerge that could

---

4 The Scottish Christian Aid Committee (SCAC) is made up of staff members and of representatives from the various churches and groups who support Christian Aid in Scotland.

influence both the practice of development and the practice of liberation. I situate the theologies of development and liberation in their space and time, from their origins to the possibilities for the future.

There are Christians involved in the practices of development and liberation around the world, yet it is not always clear to us what is distinctive about Christian practice. Is it different from secular practice? If so, how? How do development and liberation differ?

There are several ways to begin this discussion. People involved in development work, particularly in the North,[5] may not see the point of mixing faith and development. Yet, often people practising development or liberation in the South do not formally separate their faith from other aspects of their lives, such as economics and politics. Their practice of development or liberation includes spirituality and their spirituality pervades their economics and politics. This overt mixture can also help us to understand the linkages that may be hidden in the practice of many of us in the North.

I began my thought process on the side of development and only through listening to those who live in the South did I begin to understand the other side of the argument. The theologies of development cannot answer the deeper questions that the theologies of liberation ask, based on the experiences of those who are oppressed. When we are satisfied

---

5 What do I mean by the North and the South? I use this language to differentiate between countries like the USA or Europe, for example, and 'poorer' countries around the world. This is an awkward and imprecise distinction to make and scholars have used different terms throughout the past 50 years. One common set of terms is West and non-West, but that defines people in terms of who they are not. People have also used the terms First World and Third World to distinguish between the richer and poorer countries. Yet, that terminology developed in a time when there was a Second World, during the Cold War. After this period, the terminology changed again to distinguish between a First World and a Two-Thirds World, which does emphasize well that those who live outside the 'West' are a majority of the world's population. However, precedence is implied by 'First' World. I prefer the terms North and South, although they are vague and in some instances, like Australia or Mexico, completely incorrect! In the majority, it is geographically apt and does not assign privilege to one over the other within the words themselves.

with development we neglect our calling to work toward this new heaven and new earth.

This opinion will only be of use to you as you come to understand the process that the people working to create, define, and practice theologies of development and liberation went through. I do not expect you to come away from the concluding chapter agreeing with every point. However, I hope the series of issues presented in this book will help you engage seriously with the questions about faith and justice we face in daily life.

At each stage, we'll look not only at the issues that emerge from the discussion but also at how people proceed in these discussions, as the methods they use are different. Deciding how to approach the questions is just as important as the answers we find. There is less written on theologies of development than on theologies of liberation and they have less impact on the North than on the South. This makes sense, as the majority of Christians in the South struggle on a daily basis to survive, and must work to answer the questions posed by this struggle in daily life. For example, in Brazil, in contrast to the USA and Europe, only 6 per cent of the population would be considered middle or upper class.[6] Thus, the base from which Christians believe and act is different.[7]

---

6 Estimates of Brazil's poverty vary widely. World Bank statistics, for example, state that the top 20% of the population has 64% of the total country income while the bottom 20% holds 2% (World Bank, 2005). Thus, inequality is severe. What is certain is that the poor and marginalized continue to form the majority of Brazil's population. Marshall Eakin, professor of Latin American History, estimates 60% of the population live in poverty in Brazil making the minimum wage or less (currently $177/£90 per month). They are excluded from the global capitalist economy. The next 34% of the population are considered the working class, making at least twice the minimum wage. The middle and elite classes make up only 6% of the population. For further information on the class structure in Brazil, see Eakin 1997. For those who read Portuguese, see Costa, 2002. The situation is worse in particular regions. In Bahia, for example, only 60.5% of the population is employed. Twenty-four per cent of 10–14-year-olds in Bahia work, much worse than the national average of 9.7%. Forty per cent of those who work live in families who receive less than one half a minimum salary per person (Guimarães, 2001).

7 Seventy-five per cent of Brazilians define themselves as Roman Catholic.

The next diary excerpt is set in Gamboa de Baixo, one of the local communities with which *Centro de Estudos e Ação Social* (CEAS)[8] works. CEAS is a CSO located in Salvador,[9] a city halfway up the east coast of Brazil. Salvador was one of the main ports for importing slaves into South America, and retains a population that is around 90 per cent Afro-Brazilian or mixed race. CEAS helps communities in their struggle to survive, finding their place in the global situation and then analysing and critiquing this situation from its faith base in order to move forward. It is a small organization[10] working in and around the city and region. It receives funding from other larger organizations including Christian Aid.

Gamboa de Baixo is located on the side of cliffs on coastline near the centre of the city of Salvador. It is made up of 250 families, some of whom have lived in this area for more than 80 years. For the last 30 years they have been under the threat of losing their land, particularly after the construction of a new main road at the top of the cliff, which cuts them off from the city centre. To reach the community, one has to climb down underneath this road, as it juts out over the steep incline. The government has tried to expel the people from the area in order to develop an official tourist programme. However, the community has been successful in legally defending its right to the land.

---

Another 20% consider themselves to be Protestant, mainly evangelical. The remaining 5% align themselves with the various strands of Afro-Brazilian religions, in Bahia's case mainly Candomblé. The Afro-Brazilian religions combine elements of Roman Catholicism with traditional African religions. Nearly the entire population identifies with some variant of Christianity. See http://www.cesnur.org/testi/irf/irf_brazil99.html for further details.

8  CEAS, Centre for Studies and Social Action, is a Brazilian Jesuit-based civil society organization.

9  Extreme economic wealth and poverty exist side by side. Salvador has over 2,000,000 people, a petrochemical industry, a large civil service, a university, and a hugely expanding tourist sector (Kraay, 1998). Nearly 38 out of every 100,000 people in Salvador are murdered each year. Half of the people in the state of Bahia have no access to clean water. Around 60% of Salvador's inhabitants live in informal (not legal) situations, rising to 73% if only habitable areas are considered. These statistics come from CEAS.

10  It has 20 staff members, four of whom are Jesuits.

The following excerpt from my research diary describes a meeting between two of CEAS's staff members and the community residents' association. The group was planning for a visit to the community by some representatives of the local media. This event was seen by the community to be critical to their ongoing survival. The residents' association is advised by CEAS and they meet together twice a month in an ongoing effort to improve the lives of those in the community.

## 'Talk fast because I am hungry': Fieldwork diary, Salvador, Brazil, 24 July 2001[11]

I met Rita Santa Rita, the director of CEAS, at the office around 5.30 p.m., just as the sun was starting to set. She was running a bit late it seemed, so I spoke for a few minutes with one of their newer staff members, Zé. He had a constant smile, very short brown hair, and light brown skin. When Rita arrived, she had a big grin on her face and her long dreadlocks were partially tied back. She joked that she had given us an earlier time for the meeting, so we'd be on time. We walked together to the bus stop at the end of the road and then rode the bus to Campo Grande, a large palm-tree-lined square where most of the city buses begin or end their routes. She said we'd walk the rest of the way as she wanted to stop off and buy some dinner for all of us who would be at the meeting. She went into a nearby bakery and when she returned, I saw that dinner consisted of buttered rolls.

At the end of a wide paved road, overlooking the ocean, we climbed down a set of concrete steps. I could not see where the steps led, although I could hear the crashing of the waves, as by this time it was completely dark and the path was unlit. We emerged from under the other side of a busy carriageway and on to a dirt path that ran down the steep slope from the carriageway behind us, presumably to the water, although I could not

---

11 To ensure the safety of the people in the communities with which CEAS works, all their names have been changed and I will not provide descriptions of the members of the residents' association.

see that far. Several young boys stood at the foot of the steps watching us and Rita greeted them and walked past. We made our way along the underside of the bridge, through rubble, bits of concrete that had fallen off the bridge and other garbage I could not identify by the moonlight, to a community of 250 families called Gamboa de Baixo.

CEAS has worked with this community for several years, first in their fight to keep ownership of the land on which they live and now advising as the community builds its capacity to interact with the local government. The World Bank[12] provided funding for the restoration of the area for tourism, which at first seemed to be a victory for the local government. However, when the government planned to evict the residents and relocate them on the outskirts of the city, advisers found a clause in the World Bank document, which required the government to provide accommodation for the residents in the same place.[13] Although the community is adjacent to the tourist centre, it is seen as a separate entity into which the tourists do not venture due to the perception of violence and poverty. It is also effectively cut off from the rest of the city physically. The situation is still extremely tense with frequent accusations of police violence on the one side and drug use and trafficking on the other.[14]

The squelching of our sandals in the mud was disturbing as a strong stench of sewage rose up from the ground. As we moved further down the pathway into the groupings of houses, I could vaguely make out the ocean and a few fishing boats at the bottom of the ridge. Here and there

---

12 The World Bank, created in 1944, is a group comprised of the International Bank for Reconstruction and Development and the International Development Association, along with three other organizations. See www.worldbank.org for details.

13 Following their legal success, there is now the problem of holding on to the land. 'The unemployment situation which is made worse by the lack of places in schools and by urban violence, means that selling ones home is a favourable option' (Gamboa da Baixo, 2000, p. 2). Often selling the land appears to be the only option in the short term to guarantee the survival of a family. Yet that would split the community, benefiting only the individuals who sell the land.

14 There is a drug trafficking problem in the community, which seems to be the only way to generate income, except for a small fishing fleet.

were long ropes tied from solid objects at the top of the cliff around the few trees that stood at varying levels along the slope. The rains can wash the trees down the steep slope, crushing everything in their paths. One house had been destroyed recently and there was a death from a similar incident in the previous year. We walked past several concrete shells that I took to be houses and came to a small open area, with a pay phone, a stall of traditional Bahian foods, and the smell of palm oil in the air. Preta, a woman in the late stages of pregnancy, ran the stall. Several people walked by as we descended, often greeting us, nearly all a mixture of African, indigenous American, and European descent, including a thin young girl holding a baby. Rita stopped and spoke to her for a few moments asking how she was and then told me that she was 13 and that the toddler was her baby.

Toward the bottom of the slope, we stopped at the house where the meeting was to be held. We walked down ten more steep steps into a cement patio area that held a plastic table and chairs. The house bordered two sides of the patio, the steps another and then the fourth side had several tall potted plants along the edge with what seemed to be a hole in the corner. I think it led to another house below us.

Five women and one man were present for the entire meeting and were vocal throughout the discussions. Others came in and out at various times and briefly participated in whatever was occurring at that moment. This group meets twice a month to discuss problems in the community and to co-ordinate action on the issues raised. Before the meeting came to order, several participants talked about the anti-globalization protests in Italy that were in the news at the moment, expressing their support for the protestors and dismay at the death of one.

The residents decided that the main item on the meeting agenda should be finalizing plans for a photographic walkabout. They had invited photographers and reporters from various newspapers, magazines and radio stations to spend a day visiting their community, allowing the media to see first hand what life is like for them. The reason, they said, is that the papers print what the police and the local government report, always negative accounts. When they call the papers themselves, they are ignored.

The residents had already picked out a few photographs to use as promotional material and were working on captions to go with them. One, a picture of the community's centre, stated, 'from here I am not leaving; from here no one can take me away', describing their ongoing fight to remain a community. Another read, 'watch out people, here comes *Via Náutica*'. Rita explained to me later that this is the name of the tourism plan that the local government and a company called CONDER have formed. *Via Náutica* plans to build a pier covering most of the community for boats to embark and disembark close to the main road above. The pier would destroy part of the community and at the same time would keep tourists 'safe' by allowing them literally to walk over these people to enjoy the water and then enter the centre of the city directly.

After creating these captions, the group discussed ideas for the debate with which they wanted to begin the walkabout. The first suggestion was to focus on the problems they were having with the police. The women in particular described their fear of police attacks, which augment their general fear for their safety. One woman described the most recent attack on the community in which about 40 masked people in police uniforms entered several of the houses and assaulted residents. The residents reported this incident to the newspapers, along with the licence plate number of one of the cars in which the people had arrived but nothing appeared in the news. Three of the residents ended up in hospital. Maria, a member of the residents' association, then turned to me and described the situation further. She said one mother, for example, has a son who is involved in the drug trade. The police have never arrested or talked with the son directly. Instead, they have beaten up the mother and her other son, a 10-year-old, developmentally disabled boy.

The group decided, for the debate, to present evidence showing the lack of structural support the community has from the police. They want to point out that this is made worse by the failure of the local government to work with them and by the media's refusal to report their perspective as well as that of the police. Their stories show how the police add to the violence in their community instead of protecting them from it, and how the government refuses to alleviate some of their desperate poverty by providing basic services.

I found it difficult to listen to this conversation, to hear the repeated stories of beatings and other violence. I understood why there might be people waiting at the entrance of the community, as lookouts. Yet, in the face of this grim conversation, they were still joking and laughing. As the decision for the debate topic was made, Andres, another member of the residents' association, held up a piece of paper that said 'talk fast because I'm hungry'. Rita passed around a plate on which she had put the rolls with butter. So, the serious talk ended and the second part of the meeting, our dinner of bread and butter together, began. When the last slice was gone, the meeting ended and several of the residents walked with us in the dark back to the edge of the community, where we again clambered up the steep steps in the dark to the main road . . .

CEAS, from its experiences in communities such as this one, rejects the term 'development' in two senses: its current definition and its actual process. Remember that a common definition of development is economic growth with poverty reduction. CEAS does support poverty reduction. However, development's focus on economic growth does not lead toward poverty reduction. For CEAS, development means economic growth (through the capitalist economic system) with increased economic, political, racial, gender, sexual, environmental and other types of poverty. The development work of clearing the Gamboa community from the land would break up their community, disperse them to favelas on the outskirts of the city, and thereby increase at a minimum their economic, political and environmental poverty. The definitions of development are amorphous and confusing and change over time. I will clarify these uses throughout the book.

When used in a positive context, development is often defined according to what people hope will occur, not what actually is occurring. This is the definition we see in evidence at Christian Aid. Gilbert Rist, a professor of development studies, calls these definitions 'wish lists'.[15] The term 'development' needs to describe the actual situation. Poverty may not be reduced by economic growth; instead, it may increase.

---

15 See Rist's *The History of Development*.

The dictionary definition of the word 'development' is, actually, 'the act, process or result of developing',[16] whether these results are positive or negative. Poverty reduction may be one interpretation of the results, but it shouldn't be used in the definition if it is not a universally agreed upon result. Economic growth can be used as part of the definition, at the moment, because all sides agree that it is part of the process of development.[17]

To summarize: a common definition of development in the North is *economic growth with poverty reduction*. A common definition of development in the South is *economic growth with increased economic, political, racial, gender, sexual, environmental and other types of poverty.*

Rejecting development, some people in the South began calling for liberation. Not only does development not achieve freedom from poverty but development emphasizes negative freedom: freedom from. What about positive freedom: freedom to?

What is liberation? Liberation includes both negative and positive freedoms. First, liberation requires freeing from oppression, a negative freedom. For example, it requires freedom from the global capitalist system and the forms of poverty listed above. It rejects oppression in all its forms, including development.[18] Importantly it is also freedom to act, a positive freedom. Liberation searches for alternatives that end economic, political, and cultural (etc) oppression. It focuses on empowerment: enabling the poor to free themselves, to act to better their lives.

Development and liberation (for those in favour of liberation) are opposites. People who are poor need liberation from development as well as other forms of oppression. Yet, some practitioners in the North co-opt the language of liberation and use it to try to achieve development. I'll explore this range of meanings throughout the book.

---

16 These definitions came from www.m-w.com.

17 Yet, the policies of development could change to prioritize something other than economic growth. Economies could develop qualitatively rather than quantitatively or the focus could shift to changes in the political or social realms.

18 Development, in this context, is both a form of oppression and a cause of oppression.

What is theology? I begin with the traditional understanding spoken by Anselm: faith seeking understanding. Yet this definition leaves us with a question: what is faith seeking an understanding of? Faith is seeking an understanding of God for the afterlife *and* the here and now. This emphasis on the here and now is central to political theology.

While this book is far too short to trace the history of political theology,[19] I want briefly to address its distinctiveness. Christian theology has dealt with political and economic themes since its inception. Christ, in his life, lived under a Roman political system that oppressed and exploited the Jewish population. He saw the merging of economics, politics, and religion in the doorway to the temple.[20] However, some Christian theologies have focused on the death and resurrection of Jesus as spiritual referents, moving away from the economic and political aspects of his life on earth.[21]

Political theology has focused on the political, economic and cultural aspects of Jesus' life, death, and the meaning of his resurrection. Jesus' life can be seen as a critique of the systems on earth, which will be replaced by a new heaven and a new earth. 2 Peter states 'But we look for new heavens and a new earth according to his promise, in which righteousness is to abide' (3.13). Political theology does not reject the spiritual realm but argues that the material realm is equally important. There will be a new heaven and a new earth, not just a new heaven.

In seeking this understanding in the here and now, theology is active. Theology puts faith into action. Your theology is determined not by what you say you believe, but what you do with those beliefs. Theology then is never neutral. It demands that a stance be taken on all issues. Theology deals with reality and is developed from reality. Therefore, theology is always political.

---

19 For a general discussion of the history and spectrum of political theologies and their foremost contributors see Peter Scott and William Cavanaugh, eds, *The Blackwell Companion to Political Theology*.

20 Matthew 21.12-17; Mark 11.15-19; Luke 19.45-46; John 2.13-17.

21 For example, theologies of atonement focus on Jesus Christ's death as atonement for human sinfulness.

In the contexts of development and liberation, faith is seeking an understanding of poverty in all its forms.[22] Theologies of development and liberation are two forms of political theology, which deal specifically with poverty. This book deals with their emergence, formalization, and their theory and practice today.

How do the two diary excerpts relate to the theologies of development and liberation? The communities in Scotland and Brazil put faith into practice in differing ways. Christian Aid, accepting the concept of development, works to achieve the outcomes of poverty reduction and economic growth. In its literature and in conversations with its staff, Christian Aid often argues that it is working from a perspective of liberation theology. However, its policies are often supportive of development and deal with themes that should arise in the theologies of development. The problem is that these theologies have remained stagnant. Where the theologies of liberation have their spokespeople, the theologies of development do not. Yet, people put faith into action in different ways all along the spectrum, even when there is a lack of 'formal' theology. Although the theologies of development and liberation lead to opposite conclusions, they are sometimes merged messily on the ground. This messy merging leads to messy outcomes, as we'll discuss later.

CEAS's context is very different to that of Christian Aid. In 1964, a military coup overthrew Brazil's democratically elected government. This military dictatorship did not allow dissent or political discussion and intensified the focus on policies of economic development. Many Brazilians, including the staff at CEAS, associate policies of economic development with repressive dictatorship and unresponsive govern-

---

22 Throughout this book, I'll use the terms 'theology' and 'faith' interchangeably. Sometimes the word 'theology' invokes a very formal concept for people. You might say, 'Well, I don't know much about theology, I haven't been trained.' This understanding associates theology with a formal degree, as if a theology requires systematic or dogmatic explication. If I were to ask what you believe, or ask you a question about faith, you might find it easier to respond. It seems more intuitive that faith deals with the interaction between religion (in our case, Christianity) and daily life. What we are talking about is an active theology, a 'lived theology', as one of the Christian Aid staff members said.

ment.[23] In this situation, Christian churches provided a space for political discussion and action. In 1967, CEAS was established by a group of Jesuits. Rejecting the military government and its focus on development, CEAS has always responded to direct requests from local communities like Gamboa de Baixo.

Liberation theology and the practice of agencies like CEAS grew directly out of this context of a critique of dictatorship and development. In 1984, there was a return to a more democratic rule in Brazil. Yet, the policies of economic development remain in place. Many Brazilians struggle for the democracy to become responsive to all Brazilian citizens and to end the policies of economic development.

What do liberationists want instead? Part of the answer to this question is that there is no one hegemonic outcome desired for the entire planet. On the political side, many argue for a democracy in which each citizen not only has a voice but has a voice that is heard. On the economic side, many struggle toward a just society. However, rejecting a hegemonic system is simpler than imagining its myriad local alternatives. Agencies like CEAS focus first on ensuring that the new democracy becomes relevant to Brazilian citizens. Ending poverty and encouraging active citizenship remain two crucial goals. It aims for the communities' self-empowerment, arguing that the focus should be on people as citizens rather than as consumers.

Although I use these two CSOs as examples, I acknowledge that they cannot represent every CSO. At the same time, discussions of development and liberation do not occur solely within CSOs. They take place within governments, companies, international organizations like the World Bank, churches and many other groups. In the UK, the Department for International Development (DfID)[24] provides one such example

---

23 This view can be contrasted with that of the USA or the UK where capitalist economics and democratic politics appear to go together. Several questions then arise here. Are these relationships historical accidents, or do they express causal dependencies? Are they only locally dependent, requiring certain cultural components? Theorists and practitioners on both sides disagree. Theologians also disagree, as later chapters explore.

24 See www.dfid.gov.uk for further details.

and is part of the focus of Christian Aid's advocacy. There are international organizations, including the World Bank and the International Monetary Fund (IMF)[25] that provide grants and loans to countries for development work. The World Trade Organization[26] is also a locus for these sorts of discussions. And regarding trade and consumption, much of this trade is conducted between companies. So we need to take notice of companies too: national and international and transnational.[27] For anyone of any faith, in whatever context s/he encounters these issues, there are decisions to be made.

In our discussion of these theologies, one question will appear repeatedly. Should we be focused on the economic realm, as development tends to be, or should we move beyond economics to politics, culture, etc? *Should we be focused on consumption or citizenship?*

## Chapter Outline

What are faith-based CSOs struggling toward? Christian Aid and CEAS would answer in theological language 'a new heaven and a new earth'. But what does this really tell us about development or liberation? *What should they be struggling toward?*

The first part, 'Beginnings', will describe how the theologies of development and liberation emerged and what they had to say. Chapter 1 examines the emergence of a theology of development, mainly in the North, during the 1960s. The second chapter explores the emergence of the theology of liberation in Latin America, also in the 1960s. Both theologies engaged 'development' policies from different perspectives.

---

25 The IMF was created alongside the World Bank in 1944 to promote international economic growth and stability. It also lends money to poorer countries. See www.imf.org for further details.

26 The WTO is an international organization, created in 1995, as a successor to the General Agreement on Tariffs and Trade. See www.wto.org for further information.

27 Transnational corporations (TNCs) are companies usually based in northern countries, where the profits gather, but conduct business and get the raw materials from the subsidiaries in the southern countries.

In Part 2, 'Changes', I'll explore how these theologies changed through the 1970s to 1990s. In Chapter 3, I address the stagnation of the theologies of development through the 1970s and discussions up to the present time. The fourth chapter will examine the formalization of the theologies of liberation through the 1970s and their emerging themes. I'll also explore the interaction between the two.

Part 3, 'Here and Now', will focus on how these theologies exist today, through two case studies. The fifth chapter is a case study of Christian Aid. Their advocacy was focused on the economic realm, on trade and consumption. In the sixth chapter I examine the case of CEAS. How does their practice differ from that of Christian Aid? From these cases we see liberation theologies being used today, engaging with the economic, political, and cultural realms. What does this suggest for the future of these theologies?

The final chapter, 'A New Heaven and a New Earth', asks what we should be struggling toward. I suggest that although many northern churches and agencies have co-opted the method of liberation, they would still prefer policies of development. This combination is not successful, as the method of liberation leads to a rejection of the global capitalist system and of the Northern focus on capitalism as the solution to the problems of underdevelopment. How can the theologies of development and liberation come to a compromise? Should they? What will this new heaven and new earth look like?

This short book will show these theologies and their emergence, warts and all, examining theology, politics, economics and culture. The book is interdisciplinary in nature, but theology is at its centre.

# Part I

## *Beginnings*

# 1

# A Theology of Development

## Introduction

Our discussion of the theology of development begins in the North, just as our discussion of the theology of liberation will begin in the South. These two types of political theology emerged from different experiences. The theology of development considered issues emerging from trying to alleviate *others'* poverty.

Development became a focus of northern governments after the end of World War Two. About ten years later, Christian churches began to respond to these policies of development. Christians attempted to stimulate debate over a theology of or *for* development. They asked, 'What does Christian theology have to say about development?' Their method was a monologue, not a dialogue.[1] Christian theologians suggested methods, themes and ideas for supporting development practice. Often specific policies were advocated without actual analysis of the relationship between theology and development. See Figure 1.

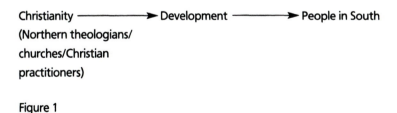

Christianity ————▶ Development ————▶ People in South
(Northern theologians/
churches/Christian
practitioners)

Figure 1

---

1 A dialogue would suggest that development itself could critique theology.

While the theology of development initially emerged to question and critique the aims and effects of development, it ended up supporting development policy. After the theology of development's initial foray, it stagnated. While it stagnated, liberation fomented in Latin America, as the following chapter considers. Development theology and policy primarily affected people in the South, generating a dialogue between northern Christianity, advocates for development, and Christians in the South. Thus, this chapter will also consider briefly the reception of the theology of development in the South.[2]

After exploring the beginnings of development theory and practice after World War Two, we will consider the following questions. Who called for a theology of development? How were they determining what the theological message should say? What was the message of the theology of development? And finally, how did the South respond to this message?

## The beginnings of development

While the policies of development formally emerged after World War Two, the tendency toward development began with colonial policies. Under colonial policies, Spain and Portugal, for example, introduced 'civilization', including a new style of economy, politics, and religion to Latin America. After the Latin American nations achieved their independence in the 1800s, local liberal elites[3] gained power. Through the early 1900s, these elites emulated the US model of society with its focus on education, capitalism, industrialization, and democracy. This

---

2 I'll specifically focus on the situation in Latin America, as this is the locus for liberation theology's emergence.

3 In this context, there was a distinction between conservatives and liberals where the conservatives tended to be rural landed elites who traditionally held economic and political power in colonial times. The liberal elites tended to be urban, involved in industry, law, business and education. At this time, the liberals urged democracy, separation of church and state and capitalist industrialization, while the conservatives favoured the colonial system with its feudal economy and close ties between church and state. These distinctions change over time.

world-view assumed there were advanced or 'civilized' nations in the North, which were in some way (economically, politically, culturally) ahead of those in the South. As development policy emerged, the new nation at the top of the pile was the USA.

After World War Two the term 'development' began to be used formally by policy makers to describe how the North could help the South.[4] The USA took its successful economic model for European recovery[5] and extended it to countries in Latin America and around the globe. In his 1949 inaugural address, US President Truman stated:

> We must embark on a bold new program for making the benefits of our scientific advances and industrial progress available for the improvement and growth of *underdeveloped* areas ... For the first time in history, humanity possesses the knowledge and skill to relieve the suffering of these people ... The United States is pre-eminent among nations in the development of industrial and scientific techniques ... In cooperation with other nations, we should foster capital investment in areas needing *development* ... The old imperialism – exploitation for foreign profit – has no place in our plans. What we envisage is a program of *development* based on the concepts of democratic fair-dealing. All countries, including our own, will greatly benefit from a constant program for the better use of the world's human and natural resources ... Greater production is the key to prosperity and peace. And the key to greater production is a wider and more vigorous application of modern scientific and technical knowledge ... Democracy alone can supply the vitalizing force to stir the peoples of the world into triumphant action, not only against their human oppressor, but also against their ancient enemies – hunger, misery, and despair. On the basis of these four major courses of action we hope to create the conditions that will lead eventually to personal freedom and happiness for all mankind.[6]

---

4 See Rist's *History of Development* for a more detailed history.

5 Part of this model included European debt relief, a controversial issue for southern countries today.

6 From Great Books Online, www.bartleby.com/124/pres53.html (italics are mine).

Truman's statement was significant for a number of reasons. First, he used the term 'development' alongside 'underdeveloped', taking 'underdeveloped' countries as a starting point and the USA as their model for the future. Underdevelopment became a term used to describe countries with 'inferior' economic and political systems. Suddenly, more than half of the world's population had a new label: underdeveloped.

Second, development, Truman argued, required both capitalism and democracy. Economically, countries in the South should follow the example of the USA: industrialize through capitalism. For Truman, this economy required democracy. This concurrent goal of democracy disappeared during the 1960s and reappeared again in the 1980s. In between, security was prioritized over democracy: securing capitalism.[7]

Third, Truman distinguished this era of development from the previous colonial period. In the colonial period, economic development in the colonies was for the benefit of the colonizing nation itself. In contrast, development was not solely for the benefit of the already developed nations. However, he did still include the point that development in southern countries was good for the USA too.

After this speech, the use of the term 'development' quickly became common among economists, politicians and others. Theorists and practitioners alike agreed that there were many countries around the world that needed to be brought up to US economic and political standards. Policy-makers in the USA and Europe, with the support of the middle and upper classes in Latin American nations,[8] aimed to achieve development.

In the UK, the history of the Department for International Development (DfID) shows this transition from the colonial period clearly.[9] DfID traces its roots back to the UK Colonial Development Act of 1929. Through time, it became the Ministry for Overseas Development, the

---

7 US presidents after Truman supported many undemocratic governments in their quest for economic development because they were pro-capitalist and anticommunist.

8 Remember they are a minority.

9 See the DfID website for further details.

Overseas Development Association and finally DfID in 1997. While its policies may have changed, the underlying theme of responsibility for the progress in the 'colonies' remains at the heart of its charge.

Development initially aimed to raise the nations in the South to the level of the North: economically, politically, and culturally. As time passed, however, the focus of policy and discussion in the North tended to narrow. It started to focus on the economic realm and more specifically, on capitalism. Thus, what was called development in the South was called capitalism[10] in the North.

Development theory (and its subsequent theology) made three assumptions. The first was that poor people needed development; they needed assistance from others to bring them out of poverty. Second was that we all shared the same definition of poverty. Third was that economic growth would lead people from poverty. Because development made these three assumptions, the political discussions that followed were subsumed under economics. Development became defined as economic growth with poverty reduction. The political component disappeared. Development assumed implicitly and often explicitly that the economic growth sought was necessarily fuelled by capitalism.

What is capitalism? Capitalism can be defined as 'an economic system characterized by private or corporate ownership of capital goods, by investments that are determined by private decision, and by prices, production, and the distribution of goods that are determined mainly by competition in a free market'.[11] Capitalism requires three foci: the individual, profit, and growth. Adam Smith,[12] in *The Wealth of Nations*, argued that individual consumers and producers were self-interested. For him, individuals wanted ever more goods and services, and their desires (and perhaps needs) were unlimited. Producers constantly wanted to increase profits from production. Thus, there was always a middle point at which these two sets of desires intersected.

---

10  It is now referred to as a 'capitalist democracy' or 'democratic capitalism'.

11  *Merriam-Webster Online Dictionary*, www.m-w.com.

12  Adam Smith (1723–90) was a Scottish philosopher, considered to be the foundational thinker in modern economics.

Capitalism focuses on profit instead of production for a basic level of subsistence. As newer technologies become available, people produce more with fewer inputs of labour and materials, so profit increases. Capitalism assumes that economies constantly need to grow. There must therefore not only be profit but this profit must constantly increase.

Those who argued in favour of development assumed the capitalist economic system would provide growth, which would then bring about poverty reduction.[13] These pieces together formed the model for development. Capitalist economies were based on private production and consumption. The state played a varying role, enabling and facilitating this process when necessary. See Figure 2.

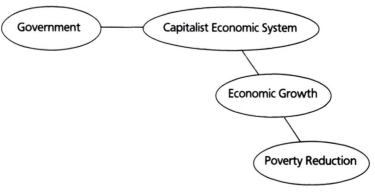

Figure 2

Development prioritized economic growth through capitalism and thus prioritized profit and the individual. The assumption that the capitalist economic system was good for individuals led to an interesting divergence. Development (and capitalism) focused on the system, assuming it brought about good for individuals. What was (and still

---

13 This is paradoxical. Under capitalism, growth is required. There is always a need for more; there is always relative poverty. The baseline will always be increasing. The global capitalist economy is not focused on absolute poverty, such that growth would stop after the absolute level had been passed.

is) neglected was the middle point in this spectrum: persons in community.[14]

The definition of poverty, too, was narrowed.[15] Poverty became a term with one global definition based on economic factors. According to development theorists and practitioners, poverty was a technical problem with a technical solution. The one solution was development.

At least two major changes occurred to poverty measurement after the advent of development. First, poverty became a lack of money. Poverty had been understood in relation to one's local neighbour. Now, people defined themselves as poor in relation to this global understanding of poverty: lack of income. Second, the baseline for poverty constantly increased. The global economy focused on consumption. It assumed individuals have unlimited desires, which over time became needs. These needs required increased consumption and increased consumption required increased income.

In development, all aspects of life were subsumed into the economic realm. Development wanted the capitalist economy to define whether one is poor or rich.[16] Thus, as I explore the theology of development, I mainly discuss economics. Although the theology of development is a 'political' theology, political discussion relates to the larger economic discussion. Theologies of development tend to accept these limitations and sometimes do not see these as limitations at all.

---

14 This is the area of focus of liberation.

15 See Iranian professor of post-development and poverty Majid Rahnema's chapter 'Poverty' in *The Development Dictionary*. There he describes not only the 'four dimensions of poverty': 'the materialities', 'the subject's own perception of his condition', 'how the others view the poor', and 'spimes (socio-cultural space-times) affecting various perceptions of poverty' but he also examines the new understanding of poverty as a globally defined concept. He analyses the assumptions this new understanding makes, its requirements for response, its results, and the responses of local communities around the world to this enforced understanding.

16 Culture, politics, gender and race do not appear in this definition. They reappear in a liberationist definition of poverty.

## 'Towards a theology of development'[17]

As public policy turned toward development at the end of World War Two, Christians began to question the concept of development. With the Cold War, there seemed only one side to political theology in the 'First World': supporting capitalist democracy and rejecting communism. International development was often seen as a way to fight communism (through promotion of capitalism in countries around the world) by both the right and some of the left.[18] The prominent view in the USA, in particular, was that communism was necessarily atheistic.[19]

The beginnings of a theology of development fit this pattern. In the economic realm there was a deepening divide between the haves and the have nots, to which Christians responded. Christians began to ask whether development was a solution and, if so, what policies within development they should support.

The method Christian churches (and theologians) used in order to work toward a theology of development had six characteristics. First, they assumed theology would reflect on the process of development, as a monologue. They argued that theology could motivate people to work toward development. Theology could also help analyse goals and methods. Theology could lend advice to development. Second, economics and politics (and later development studies) were treated as technical subjects that did not require ethical discussion. Third, the development paradigm was accepted a priori: only certain aspects of development were questioned. Fourth, the three previous characteristics meant that specific development policies were accepted before theologi-

---

17 This is also the title of a bibliography published by the World Council of Churches.

18 Harvey Cox, theologian and professor, made a similar critique in his introduction to a selection of papers from a WCC conference on Church and Society in 1967, *The Church Amid Revolution*.

19 If communism were opposed to religion, it would not be an option for Christians. Yet, there were representatives from Communist bloc countries active in the World Council of Churches. It was possible to be Communist and Christian.

cal discussion occurred. Fifth, these specific policies tended to focus on the economic realm. Finally, theology and development were kept separate. Economists tended to discuss economic development and theologians theology.

Christians churches in the North wanted to tell Christians around the world how they should act and why they should act in this way. However, the 'putting together' of theology and development never seemed to occur. There remained a gap between the dogmas of the Christian churches and the specific policies of development they supported.

By 1960, discussion started to move from the East–West[20] divide to the North–South divide. One of the first to call for consideration of a theology of development was L. J. Lebret[21] who discussed the urgency for development of the world's poorest nations, addressing political and economic aspects. The following year, Paul Abrecht,[22] a World Council of Churches staff member, also published a book calling for consideration of theology and development.[23]

Following this, both the Catholic and Protestant churches undertook a discussion of development issues. In the Catholic tradition, Vatican II (1962–5) discussed, amidst other issues, the Church's role in the world reflected in *Gaudium et Spes*. In 1967, the papal encyclical *Populorum Progressio* was issued, dealing with 'the Development of Peoples'.[24] Pope

---

20 East refers to the former Soviet Union and other Communist bloc countries. The West refers to the USA, the UK, and other capitalist countries.

21 Lebret was a French Dominican, involved in development, who wrote *The Last Revolution: The Destiny of Over- and Underdeveloped Nations*. Its original title was *Le Drame du Siècle*.

22 His background included a BD from Union Theological Seminary (where he also was an instructor in Christian Ethics) and a BA in economics.

23 In *The Churches and Rapid Social Change* he treated economic and political development as separate discussions. Later books and conferences also separated economics from politics and this tendency led to the economic being prioritized and the political being sidelined, although such was not the case with this first book.

24 Interestingly, a 'note to the reader' at the beginning of the American edition qualifies the encyclical by stating that the translation was done by the

Paul VI then created the Pontifical Commission on Justice and Peace to research and work toward social justice.[25]

The WCC also began to discuss the Church's role in the world in relation to North–South issues. In 1966, a World Conference on Church and Society was held entitled 'Christians in the Technical and Social Revolutions of our Time'. The divisions that became most prominent in the conference were between participants from the North and South, not between the East and the West. According to Cox:

> Participants from those countries where some form of communism is established had no reason to feel they were outsiders. In fact, not only were the East Europeans not condemned by the West, but the two often found themselves drawn closer to each other in response to the stinging criticisms of Africans and Asians. This 'attack from the South' made the old East–West dichotomy almost irrelevant. (Cox, 1967, p. 22)

These divisions eventually led to the theologies of development on one side and liberation on the other.

---

Vatican Polyglot Press. Revd John F. Cronin of the US Catholic Conference states that 'this individualistic system of capitalism so strongly condemned by Popes Leo XIII, Pius XI, Pius XII, John XXIII, and Paul VI involves a type of calloused exploitation which certainly is not descriptive of the prevailing business practices of the United States in 1967. However, since the Encyclical is written for world-wide consumption, such warnings are indeed timely, since exploitive capitalism does characterize the economic systems of many of the poorer nations of the world.' Americans were being told before even reading the document, that the condemnation of capitalism was not relevant for them.

25  Pope Paul VI stated, 'In Our desire to carry out the wishes of the Council and give specific expression to the Holy See's contribution to this great cause of peoples in development, We considered it Our duty to set up a Pontifical Commission in the Church's central administration, charged with "bringing to the whole of God's People the full knowledge of the part expected of them at the present time, so as to further the progress of poorer peoples, to encourage social justice among nations, to offer to less developed nations the means whereby they can further their own progress"' (Paul VI, 1967, §§ 4–5).

A theology of development did not emerge from this conference.[26] There was little interaction between theology and development. Development discourse was limited to economic growth.[27] And instead of a conversation between theology and development policy, there emerged a laundry list of practices and policies Christians specifically should support.[28]

Calls for a theology of development continued. In 1968, Catholics and Protestants created the Joint Committee on Society, Development and Peace (SODEPAX) to deal with issues of development.[29] It was to be a 'catalyst' for discussion of a theology of development between the Roman Catholic and Protestant churches. Yet it took time for the conversation over theology and development to emerge. The first SODEPAX conference (Beirut 1968) focused on 'economic development'.[30] The

---

26 This was one criticism of the conference at the time. Paul Ramsey, a professor of Christian Ethics, questioned the series of pronouncements about what precisely should be done. 'Must the churches choose between abstract, pious irrelevancies and policy-making exercises?' (Ramsey, 1961, p. 28) The conference planners produced a series of four books beforehand (*Christian Social Ethics in a Changing World, Responsible Government in a Revolutionary Age, Economic Growth in World Perspective,* and *Man in Community*), which at first glance seemed to cover all aspects of a 'responsible society'. There was discussion of ethics, politics, economics, and persons in community but not theology and development.

27 There was detailed discussion of the political realm in *Responsible Government in a Revolutionary Age,* but it was not linked to development, except where it was stated that certain types of states should be supported to promote economic development.

28 There is only one short section on 'theological issues in social ethics' in the conference report. The conference split into four sections. Instead of each group integrating theological discussion with its particular focus and reporting this integration, the theological discussion was given to a separate working group. This lack of interaction between theology and development is also true of the WCC's Fourth Assembly in 1968.

29 This committee continued its work until 1980; it worked with the Catholic Commission on Justice and Peace and the Protestant Commission on the Churches' Participation in Development (CCPD) (set up in 1970).

30 The conference report noted this limitation. 'The economic problem is only one aspect of the many-faceted problem of human development. The Beirut

participants themselves were mostly economists and other 'experts' in the field of development, with a few representatives from Christian churches. These representatives were to return to the churches with advice on development matters.

Finally, in 1969, there was a consultation of 28 theologians from around the world to consider method, theology and development. This consultation produced a report called *In Search of a Theology of Development*, which reflected on starting points for theology and development and theology and liberation.[31] The report introduced questions that its authors hoped others would later answer, leading to the creation of a theology of development.

Still there was no emergence of a theology of development. Instead, a gulf remained between formal theologies and the practice of development on the ground.[32] To bridge this gap, the World Council of Churches published an annotated bibliography with source material on development theory, philosophy, Christian theology, methodology, ethics and theological issues the WCC considered useful as a starting point for a theology of development.[33]

---

conferees were . . . asked, however . . . to center their attention upon the economic factor, which, if not the whole problem, is certainly one of its most important parts' (Munby, 1966, p. ix). There was a follow-up conference in Montreal in 1969, 'The Challenge of Development', which continued this conversation. And in 1970, there was also a consultation on 'Ecumenical Assistance for Development Projects', which considered what the WCC member churches could and should do with their funding for specific development projects. In response to this consultation the WCC created the CCPD.

31  For the purposes of this chapter, we will look solely at theology and development. Yet it is important to note that even from the beginning, there were those participants who rejected development in favour of liberation.

32  In 1970, the WCC published *Technology and Social Justice*, which contained several articles from a symposium of the International Humanum Foundation reflecting on the work of the WCC between 1966 and 1968. Only one chapter deals with the subject of a theology of development: 'Introduction to a Christian Phenomenology of Development' by Nikos A. Nissiotis, a Greek professor of religion.

33  Its title was *Towards a Theology of Development*.

## Starting Points for a Theology of Development

Stagnation and confusion can clearly be seen in the emerging theology. Starting points were suggested by several groups, but the policies they addressed had already been adopted by the WCC, leaving no room for dialogue. Development policies were supported a priori but the theological support was missing. The one positive starting point that emerged from the meetings and discussions of the 1960s asked: Is development salvation? Apart from this one question, the discussion became largely critical of development, asking: What should the North do with its riches? What do the new heaven and the new earth mean for economic and political structures? Should humanity be at the centre of development? None of these questions was fully answered at the time.

WCC documents make it clear that they believed certain policies of development should be supported.

> The churches should welcome the development of science and technology as an expression of God's creative work. They also should welcome the economic growth and social development which it makes possible. (World Conference, 1967, p. 90)

> Christians should . . . support action at the national and international level in order: . . . to improve international trade patterns and practices so as to widen the opportunities for every nation, on terms fair to all . . . Christians should arouse the conscience of all men to a recognition of their human solidarity and their obligation to support the increase of development assistance. (World Conference, 1967, p. 151)

In other words, economic growth is positive. The North should help the South. Christians need to encourage fairer trade and increased aid. But why?

At the outset, both Lebret and Abrecht suggested that there were points of engagement between Christianity and development. For Lebret, 'the tragedy is that the West has, in its actions, gone back on the scale of values bequeathed to it by Christianity and which is today the scale of values that could inspire a new civilization' (Lebret, 1965, p. 90). Christianity should begin by getting Christians in the North to care about development. Thus, in the intersection between theology and development, development seemed to be supported. The question was: *why, as Christians, should we support development?*

## Is development salvation?

This question was posed (but not answered). Christians were urged to look not only at the life of Christ, but also at his death and resurrection in order to 'work for a world-wide responsible society and to summon men and nations to repentance' (World Conference, 1967, p. 51). The concept of repentance implied there was sin that needed to be repented for, but what, how and who were not specified.

Introducing the death and resurrection of Christ led to the question of salvation. 'Salvation proves here to be the depth dimension of development which is the missing element in its simple function and completion' (Nissiotis, 1971, p. 153). By re-examining the concept of development in the light of salvation, the meaning of development might become clearer. Nissiotis clarified the situation further: 'I do not simply mean forgiveness of sins . . . I mean the transfiguration and transformation, in the broadest possible meaning, of the world' (Nissiotis, 1971, p. 153). Salvation was not only to erase the sin that has been committed but to change the person. Could this twofold concept relate to development? If development were to be equated with salvation, what characteristics would it have? Others confirmed this link between development and salvation but did not expound on it.[34]

The vast majority of the theology that emerged from discussions of development was actually critical of development itself. It claimed alle-

---

34 For example, Demosthenes Savramis argued: 'New Testament theology therefore consists of the glad tidings that through the death and resurrection of Christ man can completely revolutionize and change both himself and the world in which he lives' (Savramis, 1971, p. 407). Would this be development? Or would it be closer to liberation?

giance to the concept but called into question its fundamental tenets.[35] Thus, in addition to the gap between theology and development in method there also appeared a gap between theology and development in substance.

## What should the North do with its riches?

The response to this question focused on the economic realm. Theologians repeatedly suggested not only ways to alleviate poverty, but how riches should be used. How much wealth should the North have, they asked.

> The churches have long seen the dangers of both poverty and plenty, drawing on the wisdom of the simple, unlettered man whose prayer has been preserved through the ages:
>
> > Give me neither poverty nor riches;
> > Feed me with the bread of my modest allotment
> > Lest I be full and deny Thee and say, Who is the Lord?
> > Or lest I be poor and steal and take the name of my God in vain
> > (Proverbs 30.8, 9). (Kuin, 1966, p. 36)[36]

Should both poverty and riches be alleviated? It seemed so but there was no link to policy.

This question gave rise to a second: If riches were not alleviated, how should the wealthy use their riches? *Gaudium et Spes*[37] argued, 'The Fathers and Doctors of the Church held this view, teaching that men are obliged to come to the relief of the poor, and to do so not merely out of their superfluous goods. If a person is in extreme necessity, he has the

---

35 We will see a similar trend in the case of Christian Aid now.

36 Pieter Kuin was director of Unilever Company of the Netherlands and a former economics professor.

37 *Gaudium et Spes*, published at the end of Vatican II, linked theology and practice more clearly than WCC documents. It also had a clearer critique of development.

right to take from the riches of others what he himself needs (§ 69). What would it mean for development if humans were 'obliged' to alleviate poverty from their own riches? If the poor had the right to some of these riches, to whom did they belong?

The WCC considered the same question of the riches of the wealthy but from a different angle. The Church and Society document stated, 'Man's responsibility for the vast increase in technological and scientific power needs to be explored in the light of . . . his stewardship' (World Conference, 1967, p. 205). Reconsideration of the Christian concept of stewardship of the earth's resources appeared to be necessary, but none of the writers who advocated development specified how this reconsideration would affect development policy. Theological arguments flirted with a critique but practice remained unchanged.

A third question arose from the previous two: what was the relationship between the worship of wealth and the worship of God? Christians in the North needed to make a choice between putting money[38] and economic growth first or putting God first. 'When men get richer they worship riches and forget God,' Preston wrote, seemingly questioning economic growth as well as unlimited wealth (Preston,[39] 1966, p. 107). Were Christians putting growth above all else, even God? Charles Elliott[40] suggested that 'one may ask oneself whether economic growth and economic development is not becoming a new golden calf' (Elliott, 1966, p. 339). Christians needed to return money to its proper status, 'a means and not an end' (p. 340). How was this to be done? What did this mean for capitalist development policy and practice?

---

38   This aspect was particularly difficult to reconcile, and often the passage 'the love of money is the root of all evil' from 2 Timothy 6.10 was called into the discussion – again, without resolution.

39   Ronald Preston was an Anglican ethicist, author of *Religion and the Ambiguities of Capitalism* (1993).

40   At this time, he worked with the WCC. Later he became director of Christian Aid.

*What do the new heaven and the new earth mean for economic and
political structures?*

Christian theology argued that nothing should be put before God,
neither money nor economic growth, nor any economic or political
structure. 'The Christian is therefore called to speak a radical "No" – and
to act accordingly – to structures of power which perpetuate and
strengthen the status quo at the cost of justice to those who are its victims'
(World Conference, 1967, p. 200). Yet the link between theology and
policy remained unclear. How were Christians to 'act accordingly'?

The relationship between God, Christians, and structures was
explored in two ways. First, Christians could consider how the kingdom,
God's new heaven and the new earth, could relate to our economic and
political systems. 'His Kingdom is coming with his judgement and his
mercy' (WCC, 1968, p. 45). What might that mean for economic and
political practice?

There were two contrasting ideas presented. On the one hand, there
was a warning: 'the role of the Messiah was conceived in the image of a
revolutionary leader. In refusing to be a Messiah of this pattern, the
Master clearly demonstrated for all times that his Gospel neither will nor
can conquer the world by political means' (World Conference, 1967,
p. 203). So should Christians be involved in politics?

On the other hand, a later WCC document argued: 'in their faith in the
coming Kingdom of God and in their search for his righteousness,
Christians are urged to participate in the struggle of millions of people for
greater social justice and for world development' (WCC, 1968, p. 45).
This document clearly argued that Christians should in some way be
involved in economics and politics.

How could the two ideas be merged for practice? Savramis offered
one possibility, arguing that 'the theology of the cross and of the resurrection . . . will unmask all attempts to deify political power by declaring
them to be blasphemy against both God and man' (Savramis, 1971,
p. 410). Perhaps one could argue that political power should not be
deified, but Christians should in some way participate in politics. How
this was to occur in practice still needed to be considered.

Second, the theologians related the discussion of God's kingdom to the New Testament discussion of principalities and powers.[41] The new heaven and a new earth were made possible by God defeating the principalities and powers. 'The political and economic structures groan under the burden of grave injustice, but we do not despair, because we know that we are not in the grip of blind fate. In Christ God entered our world with all its structures and has already won the victory over all the "principalities and powers"' (WCC, 1968, p. 45). God overcame the powers of this world through the death and resurrection of Christ. How does Christ's relationship with the powers in the New Testament relate to human interaction with the political and economic systems? Again, ideas were presented without direct links to the practice being advocated.

*Should humanity be at the centre of development?*

This question emerged as theologians tried to grapple with how Christ's overcoming the powers could relate to human interaction with political and economic structures. Neither money nor economic growth nor structures should be above God. Where should these structures stand in relation to human beings? 'Development cannot be limited to mere economic growth. In order to be authentic, it must be complete: integral, that is, it has to promote the good of every man and of the whole man' (Paul VI, 1967, pp. 13–14). Theologians began to argue that humans should be at the centre of development discussions, not economic growth. They presented two areas: the *Imago Dei* and love of neighbour.

First, humans were created in the image of God. If God was to be put above economic and political structures, perhaps humanity, in God's image, should be too. Preston suggested that because of our being made in the image of God, 'perhaps the underlying Christian concern is to insist that "economic growth is made for man and not man for economic

---

41 'For we are not contending against flesh and blood, but against the principalities, against the powers, against the world rulers of this present darkness, against the spiritual hosts of wickedness in the heavenly places' (Ephesians 6.12).

growth"' (Preston, 1966, p. 112). If this argument was accepted, how would development practice change?

Second, humans were commanded to love one another. Yet, this commandment to love was not discussed alone. For example, Hans-Heinrich Wolf, German economics professor, argued: 'Love as the criterion of Christian action must be translated in practice into justice even where it cannot be realized in its full dimensions' (Wolf, 1971, p. 431). Love and justice were discussed together.

Thus, third, having been made in the image of God and commanded to love each other, Christians needed to learn the definition of justice. The report from Uppsala argued, 'Christians who know from their Scriptures that all men are created by God in his image and that Christ died for all, should be in the forefront of the battle to . . . create a sense of participation in a world-wide responsible society with justice for all' (WCC, 1967, p. 45) What is the definition of justice? How should we love one another? And what would this mean for development practice? These were all important questions but they received little in the way of answers.

Many questions emerged from these starting points. The problem was that in order to answer these questions, theologians would have to give up the a priori acceptance of development. Christian churches wanted a conversation between theologians and development practitioners with Christians suggesting what should occur in development practice. Not only did theology not fully reflect on development but the reality of development itself could not speak back to theology. Concepts from theology, like Christology, the study of Jesus Christ, may have had something to say about development, but development could say nothing about the person of Christ.

Further, there was confusion over whether and how theology and the social sciences could be blended.[42] What could theologians possibly

42 It seemed natural to northern theologians to blend theology and philosophy. In fact, the SODEPAX bibliography contained not only 'sources for a theology of development' but also a section on 'the idea of progress and development in philosophy'. However, to extend theology to another field such as economics or politics made theologians pause.

say when a specialist argued that capitalism was critical for reducing poverty?

> The problem of values and value judgments in the social sciences is rarely looked at from the perspective of Christian theology. Yet the social sciences are inescapably involved in questions of value, not only interpreting data but as an inherent element in the basic presuppositions and methodology. Theologians must inevitably be concerned with the values that emerge in the work of social scientists and the role and function of social science within the domain of truth. (Muelder,[43] 1967, p. 330)

Although, Christians seemed to treat the social sciences as technical subjects with no ethical component, such was not the case. Theologians had to realize they could have something to say about economics and politics.[44] They did not have to accept the development paradigm or specific policies a priori.

## Context in the South

In the end, what emerged most strongly from these documents alongside these criticisms was a call from the South for liberation. As part of the report, *In Search of a Theology of Development*, Gustavo Gutiérrez[45]

---

43 Walter Muelder was dean of the Boston School of Theology and an observer at Vatican II.

44 The World Conference on Church and Society Official Report confirmed this need. 'If the Church is to provide its members with guidance in their service to the world, it must discover how to make possible a constant dialogue between the social scientists and the theologians, and between those who engage in the study of social problems and those who spend their time in the common tasks in society' (p. 49). The emergence of the hermeneutical circle and liberation theology answered this call.

45 He is a Peruvian theologian, one of the first to reflect formally on liberation theology.

wrote on 'The Meaning of Development: Notes on a theology of liberation'. The question he posed was whether we should aim toward development or toward liberation. He argued for liberation. 'The term liberation avoids the pejorative connotations which burden the term development. At the same time, it is the logical expression of the most profound possibilities contained in the process known as development' (Consultation on Theology and Development, 1970, p. 125). He was joined by these voices from the North also critical of development. What started as a question of whether development was salvation became a call for salvation as liberation.

The call for a theology of development met with some positive reaction, some criticism and some indifference in the North, yet its effects were felt most keenly in the South. Elite classes, supported by some of the Catholic and Protestant hierarchy, promoted policies of development, despite the gap between it and theology. As Enrique Dussel, Argentinian philosopher and theologian of liberation, argued, 'The theology of development reflected the faith that partial, social, political, and economic reforms would suffice' (Dussel, 1981, p. 325). In Dussel's view, and in the views of many other Latin Americans who would come to embrace liberation theology, partial reforms were worthless, causing more harm than good.

In Latin America, the introduction of the theologies of development followed on from theologies put forward by the Catholic hierarchy that had favoured the elite. They were not on the side of the poor and the oppressed. They did not acknowledge the Latin American perspective that underdevelopment was the direct result of the development that had taken place in the North. In the midst of this disagreement between theologians emerged liberation theology.

## Conclusion

While this chapter started with development, it ends with the beginnings of a call for liberation. In the conversation between theology and development, the critical voices were not only the most vocal but provided deeper analysis of Scripture and tradition. In the North, however, a gap remained between critical theology and the churches' support of development policy. Although theologians asked if development might be salvation, no immediate answers were found. Protestant and Catholic churches seemed to accept the implicit theology behind the explicit advice to support particular calls for development.

The method the churches and theologians used to consider theology and development failed them and liberation theology arose instead. Development itself was entering a crisis stage. The focus on development in the 1950s and 60s had given way to disillusion in many quarters. How could the Christian churches respond to this situation? What should they do? The clearest answer came from the work of theologians with communities on the ground in the South.

# 2

# A Theology of Liberation

## Introduction

Our discussion of the theology of liberation begins in the South, just as our discussion of theologies of development began in the North. The theology of liberation emerged from the experience of trying to survive in and eradicate *one's own* poverty. Where development began as a secular concept, liberation began as a spiritual and material concept.

Liberation was in part a response to the effects of policies of development, which labelled Latin America 'underdeveloped'. Christian churches in Latin America, filled with the poorest in society, formed base ecclesial communities (BECs),[1] from which sprang a new theology. The communities asked: Why are we poor? What does our situation of poverty have to say about Christianity? What does Christianity have to say about poverty? How should we, as Christians, respond to our situation?

In theological terms, the discussion in the South was very different from the theology of development. After analysing the situation of poverty and oppression, Christians in the South called for liberation from this oppression. The first shift was from acceptance of development to rejection and a search for alternatives.

The focus on communities points to the distinctiveness of the method: the hermeneutical[2] circle. In the North, theology suggested ideas for

---

1 These communities were voluntary, made up of anywhere from 15 to 100 people. The BEC bridged the gap between the individual and the parish (often with thousands of parishioners).

2 Hermeneutical means interpretive.

development and failed at interaction. In the South, a second shift occurred: theology was not a monologue but a dialogue, in which the life experience of the poorest linked directly to their faith, theological reflection, and further practice. The theologian drew together the threads of this reflection. See Figure 3.

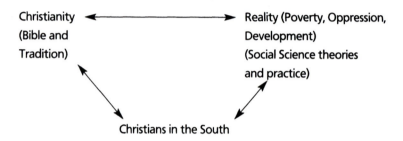

Christianity     ⟵⟶     Reality (Poverty, Oppression,
(Bible and                         Development)
Tradition)                         (Social Science theories
                                          and practice)

Christians in the South

Figure 3

This theology challenged the churches in the North to reconsider their support of development policies. First, the theology of development had not moved beyond its starting points. Second, theology was emerging from the South that strongly countered policies of development.

In this chapter, I will explain the reactions to development policies in Latin America.[3] I will then address the following questions. How did the theology of liberation emerge? What was the hermeneutical circle? What did liberation theology have to say? And finally, how did the North react?

---

3 I focus on Latin America, and Brazil in particular, for two reasons. First, liberation theology emerged from Latin America so its experience is crucial to the telling of the story. Second, this book is too short to detail the experiences of Christians in every country in Latin America. Thus, I have chosen Brazil's experience as an example. While unique in many respects, it also mirrors the situation of many other Central and South American countries.

## The Context of the Call for Liberation

From independence, most Latin American countries introduced economic policies of industrialization and capitalism. Led by Latin American elites, these countries continued to follow the emerging policies of development through the 1950s and 60s. Despite this, the situation of the majority of Latin American citizens through the 1900s remained one of economic and political poverty.

### Economic Poverty

The economically poor in Latin America are comprised of rural and urban landless people. After independence, the rural landless[4] worked the land of the rural landed elites. In the early 1900s, two events in particular drove the poor toward the cities, creating the urban landless class. First, with industrialization came the potential for jobs in the cities. Second, the rural elites started to mechanize agriculture, requiring less and less labour from the landless poor. Over time, the urban landless became a majority of the economically poor. Some urban landless, living in slums on the outskirts of the cities, were able to find low-paid work in industry. Others migrated to the cities but could not find jobs. The rural and urban landless faced myriad problems. First, they lacked food and drinkable water. Second, they lacked an infrastructure for survival: sanitation, suitable shelter, etc. Finally, they lacked health care, education and other social structures.

The situation of the poor worsened as the 1900s progressed. Industrialization initially focused on export to US and European markets. With the Great Depression and World War Two, those markets stopped purchasing Latin American goods. The poor became poorer as the rural landless were needed even less to work the land of the elites and the urban landless lost their jobs in the factories.

---

4 They formed the majority of the poor in Latin America at the turn of the century.

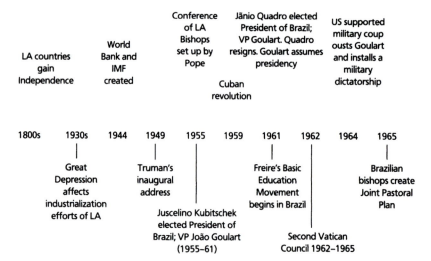

| 1800s | 1930s | 1944 | 1949 | 1955 | 1959 | 1961 | 1962 | 1964 | 1965 |
|---|---|---|---|---|---|---|---|---|---|

Above timeline:

LA countries gain Independence

World Bank and IMF created

Conference of LA Bishops set up by Pope

Jãnio Quadro elected President of Brazil; VP Goulart. Quadro resigns. Goulart assumes presidency

US supported military coup ousts Goulart and installs a military dictatorship

Cuban revolution

Below timeline:

Great Depression affects industrialization efforts of LA

Truman's inaugural address

Juscelino Kubitschek elected President of Brazil; VP João Goulart (1955–61)

Freire's Basic Education Movement begins in Brazil

Second Vatican Council 1962–1965

Brazilian bishops create Joint Pastoral Plan

The realization by the elites that this form of industrial capitalism might not bring about sustained economic growth was matched and intensified by the realization of the poor that their economic poverty was not reduced.[5] During the 1950s, the majority of Latin American elites saw development as a solution, if capitalist industrialization would shift its focus to Latin American rather than European markets, a period of import substitution.[6] They adopted part of the US position but criticized the focus on the USA and modified it to benefit Latin American countries themselves.[7]

---

5 Critics have argued that by adopting the 'colonial' policies of the North, the Latin American elites were creating an 'internal colonialism' in countries of the South.

6 Raul Prebisch, Argentine economist, argued the following. Latin America exported mainly raw goods and materials and had to import manufactured goods from the USA and Europe. It took a lot more exporting of the former to be able to import the latter. Further, the prices of raw materials and goods fell further and faster than those of the manufactured goods. So Latin America was disadvantaged. See Prebisch's *The Economic Development of Latin America and its Principal Problems*.

7 This change marks the first of several critiques of capitalism and later development. See Kay's *Latin American Theories of Development and Under-development*.

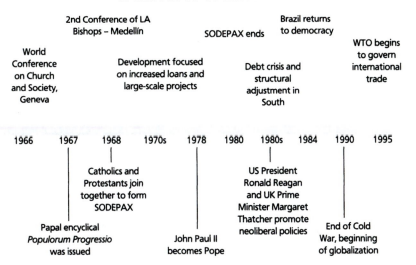

By the 1960s, however, a second critique was emerging. Policies of development were failing in Latin America. Dependency theory emerged.[8] Dependency theory argued that underdevelopment was not a starting point, as the North suggested. Rather, it was an end point, caused by the development of the North.[9] See Figure 4a. The situation was not as simple as Truman had portrayed it.

Figure 4a

<hr />

8 For details of this theory see Frank's *Capitalism and Underdevelopment in Latin America*. Andre Gunders Frank was a German economist who worked in Chile.

9 For example, Spain and Portugal had developed because of their exploitation of the Latin American countries. The USA continued this exploitation by promoting industrialization in Latin America for export to the USA and Europe. Because of this exploitation, these countries were now underdeveloped.

Some Latin Americans took on a different definition of development: *development was capitalist economic growth with increased economic, political and social poverty.*[10] See Figure 4b. The question was: what should Latin Americans do? What alternative to capitalism could be found? Could Latin America even be talked about as needing 'one' solution? Did Latin America need liberation? The discussion expanded to the political realm.

South-Economic Development (Capitalist Economic System)

| South-Economic Growth | South-Poverty Increase | North-Economic Growth |

Figure 4b

*Political Poverty*

The Great Depression and World War Two caused some elites to lose both economic and political power. Urban industrial workers began to unionize. This combination caused social and political instability among the middle and elite classes. Throughout Central and South America there were frequent shifts between democracy and dictatorships in various forms. The majority of citizens had no control over these shifts and often had no greater say in government, whichever the current model.[11] In this situation the economically poor also suffered from political poverty.

Then in 1959 the Cuban revolution took place, overthrowing the Batista regime. Cuba began to follow a socialist economic model. This sent shockwaves through the USA. Many of the former economic and political elites in Cuba left, emigrating to the USA and other countries, as they lost their land, money, and political positions. This loss also

---

10 Later definitions include race, gender, sex, culture, and environment.

11 Remember that the majority of citizens were not members of either the middle or elite classes.

worried many Latin American elites who held economic and political power. They saw that not only was development not currently alleviating poverty, but the masses seemed to be leaning toward socialist or even communist economic policies. And with the Cuban revolution, the elite saw that neither capitalism nor democracy were givens in Latin America.

In response, the USA, in concert with many of these elites, began to support dictatorship over democracy throughout Latin America, wherever democracies leaned toward socialist economic policies. In Brazil, for example, a democratic election in 1955 elected Juscelino Kubitschek president of the republic with João Goulart as vice-president. Kubitschek strongly promoted policies of development, while Goulart was known for his leanings toward redistributive policies. Together they remained in power until 1961. After another democratic election, Jânio Quadro was named president, with Goulart again as vice-president. In a strange twist, Quadro resigned six months later, leaving Vice-President Goulart in charge. Over the next few years Goulart attempted to put in place redistributive policies, increasing his unpopularity with elites and the USA. The USA accused him of heading toward a communist dictatorship. Finally, in 1964, a US-supported military coup[12] headed by General Humberto Branco overthrew this democracy, installing a military dictatorship. The military[13] government focused on capitalism and policies of development and retained the support of the USA.

Taking on the language of the USA, the Brazilian government argued it was defending 'Western Christian civilization'. It assumed it had the support of the Catholic Church. There appeared to be only two perspectives: the Christian Democratic West and the Atheist Communist East.[14]

---

12 For details of the US support, see http://www.gwu.edu/~nsarchiv/NSAEBB/NSAEBB118/index.htm, which includes links to recently declassified audiotapes and CIA documents. This article is part of the National Security Archive at George Washington University.

13 The military's purpose changed from external defence to keeping the country itself under control, politically and economically: national security.

14 Note that while democracy is a political system, communism, as countered by the West, is an economic system. It would be more accurate to say Capitalist West and Communist East as both types of economies had some dictatorships.

In its view, the military had to be in power because the West was at war with communism. There seemed to be no option for Christians but to support military dictatorship and capitalist development.[15]

Yet, within each Latin American country suffering under military rule there were movements against the repression. Regardless of what reforms or changes the movements called for, they were labelled guerrilla, terrorist, and communist by their own and the US governments. The governments made no distinction between those who simply called for an end to repression, those who called explicitly for democracy (political change), those who called for socialism (economic change), etc. For example, Brazilian Bishop Helder Camara[16] was labelled a communist despite calling for an alternative to both capitalism and communism. He wanted to address what he saw were the larger problems of North/South and rich/poor.

Instead of being able to have a debate over or analysis of policies of political and economic development, countries in the South were once again forced into the categories decided by the North. One was either a capitalist or a communist. To reject development or to critique development was to be a communist, even though the labels did not fit. The North–South divide was not the focus.


## The Emergence of Liberation Theology

How did Christians in Latin America respond to this situation? The Catholic and Protestant churches slowly moved from the side of the elites to the side of the poor. Where development emerged as a secular concept first, and the call for theology second, liberation theology and practice emerge together as Christians across Latin America reflect theologically on their situations and put into practice this reflection. Liberationists

---

15  This is despite the fact that there are Christian communists and socialists.

16  His experience is explored further in this chapter. Camara had been politically active for years and served as a church spokesman in connection with political parties that included church rights in their programme. He also served as Minister of Education.

considered Marxism, socialism, communism and other alternatives to capitalism. However, liberation theology was never wedded to any of these.[17]

In colonial times, the Catholic Church in Latin America had a close relationship with the Spanish and Portuguese governments.[18] Bishops and priests were part of the landed elite and either came directly from Spain and Portugal or were of Portuguese and Spanish descent. After independence, most of the new nations separated church from state.[19] Consequently, the Catholic churches needed to redefine their role in the lives of the people. Their response was to continue to support the elites. In the early to mid-1900s, the Church promoted Catholic Action, which aimed at a Christian democracy.[20] Catholic Action advised Catholics to See, Judge, and then Act. Elite Catholics were expected to watch what

---

17 I do not focus on socialism or communism because the focus of my argument is on the controversy between theologies of development and liberation. Where development began as a secular concept, to which the churches reacted, the calls for liberation emerged from communities on the ground as an integration of spiritual and material aspects. While socialism and communism were considered among the search for alternatives, there was never one call, one solution, demanded. Those calling for liberation, like Camara, rejected the hegemony of both capitalism and communism.

18 The Pope gave power to the Spanish and Portuguese governments to control the sending of bishops, priests, and missionaries to the Americas. The Catholic Church in Latin America was subordinate to the colonial powers. Spain and Portugal then interacted with Rome. The Catholic Church seemed to be part of the public realm in Latin America.

19 Suddenly the Catholic Church lost its cultural and political power. In many cases, the new states also expropriated the lands that the churches had owned. It is estimated that the Catholic Church in Mexico owned between one-fourth and half of all real estate at the time of independence. From independence through the 1900s, the Latin American Catholic Church also lost priests and bishops, as many returned to their native countries (Spain and Portugal).

20 In order to ensure Latin America remained a 'Christian' continent, they wanted Catholics to push forward the Church's agenda (democracy and development) in the public realm. They targeted youth in particular: university students and urban workers. The urban workers were seen as the future middle classes, and the university students were the future elites.

was happening in the world around them, to judge this based on the Church's advice, and to act on this advice. This led toward social action and consideration of the plight of the poor by many (though by no means all) middle-class parishioners, and priests and bishops too.

In the 1950s and 60s, the process of See, Judge, Act began to expand to poor Christian communities. What Catholic parishioners saw was that development policies were making the poor even poorer. The Catholic Church had to decide whether it would stay on the side of the rich or turn to the side of the poor, who made up the majority of Latin American Christians.

This conversation extended throughout the Catholic Church in Latin America in the later 1950s and 60s. In 1955, Pope Pius XII set up a Conference of Latin American Bishops that met for regular discussions with each other from that point on. Certain priests and bishops also began to live in the poor communities with their parishioners. In many countries, priests and bishops abandoned their pro-development positions and turned to actively criticizing development and military dictatorships.[21] Parishioners and priests together asked whether religion (as it existed) was an opiate of the people, as Karl Marx[22] suggested, because it sided with the elites instead of the masses. Could it be that the message of the Gospels is justice?

In Brazil in the early 1960s, bishops and priests began to call for justice.[23] In 1961, they started to promote the Basic Education Movement, grounded in the work of Paulo Freire, a Brazilian philosopher of education.[24] Further, in 1963, a group of bishops called for land reform. People

---

21 Camara's shift from calling for development to critiquing development can be clearly seen in *Church and Colonialism*.

22 Marx was a German philosopher and social scientist who worked on political economy.

23 Again, although my examples come from Brazil, the situation is repeated in countries across Latin America. Dussel's *A History of the Church in Latin America* and his edited volume *The Church in Latin America: 1492–1992* cover almost every Latin American country.

24 Freire drew on his own experience of poverty as a child and on his work with the poorest in north-east Brazil. He developed a philosophy of education, which

needed not only to be educated but to also have access to land in order to improve their lives.[25]

Freire wanted people to learn to read not only words but also the world around them – what he termed conscientization. Conscientization 'refers to the process in which men, not as recipients, but as knowing subjects achieve a deepening awareness both of the sociocultural reality that shapes their lives and of their capacity to transform that reality' (Freire, 1985, p. 93 n.2). In this process, people not only became aware of the world around them, but they understood that they could work to change this world. This self-awareness was the beginning of the process of liberation. Freire wrote:

> I recall that while I was teaching Portuguese in secondary schools in a very dynamic way, some students came to me and told me that the classes made them feel more free. They used to say to me, Paulo, now I know that I can learn! It meant undoubtedly a kind of liberation from something . . . To the extent I could prove to them that they could learn, when I challenged them, they felt more free. (Freire and Shor, 1987, p. 27)

Much of Freire's learning about conscientization, and later liberation, came from his students, whom he saw as colleagues in the learning process with him. This experience is similar to the theology of liberation emerging from the BECs together with priests and theologians in the churches. Bishops, priests and nuns learned from BEC participants and those participants in turn became self-aware. After the coup in 1964, such

---

attempted to eradicate the traditional 'banking' method of education. In the 'banking' method, the teacher delivers information to the student (making a deposit). The student memorizes information and repeats it back. In contrast, a 'problem-solving' style of education acknowledges that, while the teacher has book knowledge, the students have their life experience. All teach and learn together. See *Pedagogy of the Oppressed*.

25 We'll come back to this again in later chapters on liberation theology. We have already seen this in the case of Gamboa de Baixo in the introduction.

movements were quashed, considered to be subversive in their calls for conscientization.[26]

The military coup split the Brazilian bishops. Some argued that Christians had to support the coup because it was anti-communist. Yet, others like Camara wanted the church to confront and move beyond both capitalism and communism because neither was appropriate for Latin America. At a conference at Princeton University in 1967, Camara stated:

As long as communism appears to be the greatest of all evils; as long as the average American persists in the illusion that to die in Korea or in Vietnam is to die for the free world – an illusion because two-thirds of humanity do not belong to this free world, living as they do in destitution and sub-human conditions, and being slaves to hunger, disease, ignorance and internal colonialism; as long as the American middle class fails to understand that there are many types of socialism and many types of capitalism, to the point that Russia and the U.S. are less far apart than many ingenuous anti-communists think; as long as the American middle class is incapable of realising that the gravest social problem of our time is the ever-widening gap between the rich who get richer and the poor who get poorer; as long as there is no change of mentality, no revolution of ideas, the United States will be unequal to its immense responsibility of being the greatest democracy of our time. (Camara, 1969, p. 85)

Speaking directly to Americans, Camara argued that there was an overarching divide and it was not East–West but North–South, and within countries rich–poor. Yet, the majority of people in the North failed to see that there could be movement outside of their narrow framework.

In 1965, after Vatican II ended, Brazilian bishops created a Joint Pastoral Plan in response. This plan stated, among other things, that baptism only gave 'implicit faith' (Dussel, 1981, p. 141). The bishops argued that Brazilian Christians needed to have explicit faith, a faith that

---

26 The Basic Education Movement was halted with the military coup and Freire was forced into exile.

was both material and spiritual. Camara stated that 'to persist in a purely spiritual evangelisation would soon result in giving the impression that religion is something separate from life and powerless to touch it . . . that would support the view of religion as the opiate of the people' (quoted in Dussel, 1981, p. 198). Christianity in Brazil needed to change.

Many Brazilian priests agreed. In 1967, they wrote a letter to the bishops in which they said Brazil was '"an assassinated people" because of infant mortality, lack of daily bread and miserable salaries' (quoted in Dussel, 1981, p. 199). As priests, they wanted to respond to their people. 'We priests felt ourselves to be "prisoners", "separated from the life of the people" . . . "does not the prophetic example of Christ of fidelity to the truth not presuppose a political implication?"' (p. 199) This response would include politics, economics and all of society together. Many of these priests and bishops spoke out openly against the military government, with its focus on 'national security'. They particularly condemned the severe police repression of the poor. Camara himself refused to celebrate a Mass commemorating the military coup. He also formed a Movement for Moral and Liberating Influence.

Not all bishops reacted as Camara and these priests did. Conservative bishops formed the Brazilian Association for the Defense of Tradition, Family and Property. This Association began in Brazil and expanded to other countries including Chile. The military government and these conservative bishops together actively tried to discredit Camara and other bishops like him.

However, although the conservative bishops had the support of the government, a call for liberation was beginning to emerge across Latin America. In 1968, the second Conference of Latin American Bishops was held in Medellín, Columbia. They concluded that Vatican II reinforced their own calls for evangelization, education and reform. They found in Vatican II the support to side with the poor and to counter economic and political poverty. At the end of this conference they published a Basic Document, which reported the beginnings of liberation theology in Latin America. Although there were still many conservative bishops, the Latin American Conference of Bishops as a whole supported the call for liberation.

The conference argued that the issues for Latin America were different to those of Europe; the only choices were not capitalism or Marxism.[27] No system could be accepted when it promoted injustice and sin. It was the North–South divide that was important. They rejected the call for a theology of development and wanted to move toward 'a time . . . of liberation from every form of servitude' (quoted in Dussel, 1981, p. 145). Liberation practice and theology would go together.

In the midst of the political and economic violence and repression, a grassroots movement had swept through the Catholic churches. Base ecclesial communities were formed. The term 'base' signified they were drawn from the base of society, the grassroots, the poorest. 'Ecclesial' meant they were church-related, first emerging from the Catholic churches.[28] 'Community' meant they were not individuals 'theologizing' alone. Instead, they were groups of 15-20 people meeting together to read the Bible in relation to their lives.

BECs were promoted by the Catholic churches for several reasons. The Catholic Church wanted to find a way to keep people engaged with Catholicism. BECs were initially located in rural areas where priests visited only once or twice a year. The lack of priests encouraged the church to give laypeople more responsibility. Second, Protestantism was rapidly growing across Latin America and Catholicism wanted to counter it. Third, many priests, nuns and bishops wanted to encourage the process of conscientization.

By talking through the stories of the Bible and their lives, these communities created a new method that became known as the hermeneutical circle. As they engaged with the reality of economic and political poverty around them, they became more sophisticated in their analysis. From these discussions, liberation theology emerged.

It is only at the end of this time period, around 1970, that formal publications reflecting a theology of liberation appear. The most famous of

---

27 For details of the range of the use of Marx and Marxist thought in Latin American liberation theology, see Kee's *Marx and the Failure of Liberation Theology*.

28 They have since expanded to Protestant churches and have, in many cases, exited the confines of the churches entirely.

these is Gutiérrez's *A Theology of Liberation*, which brought together themes discussed by base communities, priests and bishops like Camara, and theologians like Gutiérrez throughout the 1960s. In particular, the new method of the hermeneutical circle was detailed. This new method achieved the creativity that those in the North calling for a theology of development were hoping for. Unfortunately for them, it rejected development and called for liberation instead.

## A Theology of Liberation

The hermeneutical circle interpreted:

1 reality in the light of faith and social science,
2 faith in the light of reality and social science, and
3 social science in the light of faith and reality.

Theological, economic, political, and cultural concepts and practices were all intertwined. Liberation theologians separated out the various aspects of the circle so they could be understood, not because they expected a community to move through them step by step. All of these aspects developed together in time and side by side.[29] Four questions were posed and answered.

1 Why are the poor poor? In the first step of this cycle, people analysed reality from the experience of the community.[30] One's own situation was examined critically, a process of conscientization. Reality had a past, a present and a future. The future would require action but the past also required analysis. So as a community analysed reality, they asked not only what was happening around them, but why was it happening, and

---

29 Marginalized populations around the world absorbed and practised something similar, as we'll see in later chapters. For example, from a feminist perspective, see Robin Morgan's *Going Too Far*.

30 For a more detailed description of the hermeneutical circle, see Althaus-Reid, 2000b; Marcella Althaus-Reid is an Argentinian feminist liberation theologian. See also the Boff brothers, Leonardo and Clodovís, Brazilian liberation theologians, and Petrella, 2006. Ivan Petrella is an Argentinian theologian.

what had led up to the present situation. The reality facing Latin Americans was economic and political poverty caused by injustice. This step was similar to the 'seeing' in the See, Judge, Act model.

2 What does this reality have to say about faith? The next step was to set reality and spirituality side by side to engage with each other. Reality as discerned and analysed became the starting point for engaging with faith or theology. Poverty had been subjected to analysis in the light of social science and history. Now faith was subjected to the same analysis. Reality spoke to faith. The Bible was contextualized by the community. This second step, along with the third, derived from the 'judging' aspect of the See, Judge, Act, model.

3 What does faith have to say about this reality? The third step was to understand how Scripture, faith and theological concepts related to the community. The analysis was done as a community, not by one theologian or priest. The community became contextualized by the Bible. Together the community intertwined the reading of reality and of faith, which led to the final step.

4 What action should Christians take based on this reflection? In this final step, reading reality and spirituality together led to action based on that reading. This is praxis: practice based on critical reflection. Yet, the circle did not end. Action continued in a circle to the first step again, reflection on the action in community. This was the 'Act' in See, Judge, Act.

Let me show this in action. The community discussing Matthew 13.31-2 in the following extract was formed by Ernesto Cardenal, a Nicaraguan priest who became a liberation theologian.[31]

Another story by way of comparison He (Jesus) set forth before them, saying, 'The kingdom of heaven is like a grain of mustard seed, which

---

31 I would ideally like to have excerpted recordings from the 1960s but people were doing and not recording or formalizing at the beginning. It's only later that theologians try to transcribe much of this material to be shared among wider audiences.

a man took and sowed in his field. Of all the seeds it is the smallest, but when it has grown it is the largest of the garden herbs and becomes a tree, so that the birds of the air come and find shelter in its branches.'

Natalia: . . . 'It seems to me that the kingdom of heaven is unity. When all of us join together and all of us love each other, that will be the kingdom of God.'

I said it was strange that for so long people believed that the kingdom of heaven was in heaven. And even today many educated Christians continue to believe this. The fact is that it was easier to think of the kingdom in the other world so as not to have to change this one . . .

William said: 'That's why he compares it with a mustard seed. Because instead of a kingdom of worldwide power, which the Jews were waiting for . . . the kingdom of Jesus is shown as a very humble little group, which goes unnoticed at the beginning: a carpenter with a few poor people. Among his disciples he didn't have one important person. Later it will also be a political kingdom that will control the earth . . .'

Teresita: 'The truth is that the kingdom belongs to the poor and that's why it's unnoticed at first. But the poor will control the world and possess the earth . . .'

Laureano: 'And the guerrilla groups are small, insignificant, poor. And they're often wiped out. But they're going to change society.'

Marcelino: 'I don't know about the mustard seed, but I do know about the *guasima* seed, which is tiny. I'm looking at that *guasima* tree over there. It's very large, and the birds come to it too. I say to myself: that's what we are, this little community, a *guasima* seed' . . . It doesn't seem either that there's any connection between some poor *campesinos* and a just and well-developed society, where there is abundance and everything is shared. And we are the seed of that society. (Cardenal, 1975, pp. 51–4)

This community reflected together on faith and reality. As communities and theologians used this method, the theology that resulted developed unique characteristics. Three of these characteristics were: praxis as the first step and theology as the second step; orthopraxis not orthodoxy; and the concept of all Christians as theologians.[32]

Theology became a second step in an active Christian life. 'Theology is reflection, a critical attitude . . . Theology does not produce pastoral activity; rather it reflects upon it' (Gutiérrez, 1974, p. 11). Theology no longer tried to tell a Christian how to act, in a monologue.[33] Rather there was dialogue between action and the theological reflection.

Theology aimed toward orthopraxis (right action) rather than orthodoxy (right rules). Although right action was the goal, both praxis and orthopraxis would continue to grow and change as reality changes.[34] The circle remained a 'hermeneutic of suspicion'.[35] Theology and action were continuously subjected to critical analysis. A community could not choose a policy and then find theology to match it. At the same time, a community could not choose a theological point and then find a policy to match.

This theology changed the definition of a theologian and re-emphasized the call to action for every Christian. Theology became *faith seeking understanding through action and reflection*. Liberation theology argued that 'God-talk' is useless without 'God-walk'.[36] There was no point to reflecting if it would not lead to action.

---

32 In the theology of development, theology spoke to development and not vice versa. Theology was primary. Second, theology was done by theologians. Further, while a theology of development was looking for right practice rather than just dogma, it did still look for dogma.

33 As the theology of development did.

34 In the same way, this book can be taken as a comment on theologies of development and liberation at this moment in time but such arguments as presented here are not set in stone, they will continue to evolve as further action and reflection takes place. This book can be used as a tool for further action and reflection in communities around the world.

35 Stemming from Paul Ricoeur, French philosopher, this concept was seen to be active in the base communities and developed by liberation theologians. See, for example, Uruguayan Jesuit priest, Juan Segundo, *The Liberation of Theology*.

36 Althaus-Reid, 2000b describes the distinction between liberation and other types of theology.

Every Christian[37] became a theologian called to act and reflect, not just those formally trained in theology. 'There is present in *all believers* – and more so in every Christian community – a rough outline of a theology' (Gutiérrez, 1974, p. 3). The task of the formal theologian was to reflect on this theology. Gutiérrez did this himself in his writing combining reflection in the communities with the tradition of the Catholic Church.

From this method, liberation theology began to focus on five themes: God working in history; theology beginning with the poor; salvation as liberation; sin as injustice; and the struggle for justice as toward God's kingdom.[38] Below I briefly describe how each theme took shape in the emerging conversation about liberation.

The concept of God working in history formed a good transition point between the characteristics of the method and the emerging themes of liberation theology, as it encompassed both. For a community to read reality and the Bible together, they must also believe that the past (the Bible) can be related to the present (reality). This concept is known as the unity of history.[39] The Bible and its message are part of history, they have a place in history. In the community discussion above, people treated the biblical text as part of history, assuming God would continue to work in history. For example, the kingdom was seen as a kingdom on earth 'when all of us join together and all of us love each other'.

Another central theme of liberation theology was that God was on the side of the poor in the Bible and in their lives now. This base community, for example, concluded that Jesus was on the side of the poor; further, the kingdom was for the poor. Gutiérrez also reflects this bias toward the

---

37 Later this concept expanded to every person, as liberation theology became multifaith.

38 Liberation theologians emphasized these points to counter the tendencies of some northern theologies to assume: 1. God worked outside of history or solely in the spiritual realm; 2. theology was neutral or overtly on the side of the rich; 3. salvation was a spiritual concept, encompassing the forgiveness of sins and providing a path to a spiritual heaven; 4. a focus on individual sin to be forgiven in order to get to heaven; and finally 5. God would bring about the spiritual kingdom alone.

39 See 'The Unity of History' in Smith, 1991, pp. 39–43.

poor. 'The whole climate of the Gospel is a continual demand for the right of the poor to make themselves heard, to be considered preferentially by society, a demand to subordinate economic needs to those of the deprived' (Gutiérrez, 1974, p. 116). He emphasized that not only did God support the poor but God liberated the poor. Quoting from a Manifesto of the Bolivian Methodist church,[40] Gutiérrez explained:

> The God whom we know in the bible is a liberating God . . . a God who intervenes in history in order to break down the structures of injustice and who raises up prophets in order to point out the way of justice and mercy. He is the God who liberates slaves (Exodus), who causes empires to fall and raises up the oppressed. (Gutiérrez, 1974, p. 116)

God was a liberator. This was the good news that should be spread to the people across Latin America. A new evangelization was required; salvation through liberation.

Liberation, for these theologians, had a much wider definition than development.[41] The goal of liberation was 'not only better living conditions, a radical change of structures, a social revolution; it is much more: the continuous creation, never ending, of a new way to be a man, a *permanent cultural revolution*' (Gutiérrez, 1974, p. 32). Liberation encompassed all realms: material and spiritual. Gutiérrez drew on the work of Paulo Freire, linking this to the process of liberation. The oppressed person 'becomes, by himself, less dependent and freer, as he commits himself to the transformation and building up of society' (p. 91). Through conscientization liberation occurred.

Liberation was salvation, according to liberation theologians.[42] 'Salvation – the communion of men with God and the communion of men

---

40 Note that this theological reflection is emerging from Protestant as well as Catholic churches and communities.

41 Remember the commonly used definition of development is economic growth with poverty reduction.

42 This question and answer is in contrast to the theology of development, which asked if development could relate to salvation but left the question unanswered.

among themselves – is something which embraces all human reality, transforms it, and leads it to its fullness in Christ' (Gutiérrez, 1974, p. 151). Liberation was salvation because it brought about communion with God and unity with each other. Christ was a saviour, a liberator, and an example of the complete merging of the spiritual and material.[43] Christ came to 'liberate all men from the slavery to which sin has subjected them; hunger, misery, oppression and ignorance, in a word, that injustice and hatred have their origin in human selfishness'.[44] People needed to be liberated from sin, this sinful poverty.[45] Justice and injustice formed part of the language of these base communities, as the above excerpt showed.

Sin was injustice, in all its forms. According to Gutiérrez: 'Sin is regarded as a social, historical fact, the absence of brotherhood and love in relationships among men, the breach of friendship with God and with other men, and, therefore, an interior, personal fracture' (1974, p. 175). Sin, injustice, broke the relationship between humanity and God. Christians could work toward justice toward salvation as spiritual *and* *material* liberation.

Liberation theologians argued that this work toward justice was work toward God's kingdom. In order to live a life of liberation, Christians needed to answer the following question. 'How do we relate the work of building a just society to the absolute value of the Kingdom?' (Gutiérrez, 1974, p. 135). The base community discussion above answered this question. Communities began to link economic and political change to a just society, God's kingdom.

When liberation theologians discussed working toward God's kingdom, they meant literally working in this world. The spiritual and

---

43 Later liberation theologians develop this theme. See, for example, Boff's *Jesus Christ Liberator* and Jon Sobrino, a Spanish Jesuit priest who served in El Salvador, *Christology at the Crossroads*.

44 Medellín Conclusions as quoted in Dussel, 1981, p. 145.

45 Gutiérrez, along with other theologians, began to emphasize material salvation in the context of creation and the Exodus story of liberation. See, for example, Spanish Jesuit Pedro Trigo's *Creation and History*. Trigo lived and worked in Venezuela. See also Croatto's *Exodus: A Hermeneutics of Freedom*. José Severino Croatto was an Argentine theologian and professor of Hebrew Scriptures.

secular realms were linked.[46] The work toward justice announced the coming of God's new earth. The kingdom was not solely a spiritual concept, but material, too. It was important for liberation theologians to keep the two balanced.

This balance was crucial to liberation theologians because it meant that even if a moment of liberation seemed secular, it had spiritual components too and vice versa. For example, Freire's Basic Education Movement, although not overtly theological, worked toward a new earth, and was a forerunner of liberation theology. Such was the case with much of the discussion in the base communities themselves.[47]

In this context, God working in history became an important theological point as well as a methodological point. It was in the reality of history that people had a relationship with God and with each other. Human beings related to God by relating to each other in the here and now. Gutierrez wrote, 'to love Yahweh is to do justice to the poor and oppressed' (Gutiérrez, 1974, p. 194). So what I did 'unto you' I was also doing 'unto Christ'. If I treated a person unjustly, I was treating Christ unjustly and so was sinning.

These themes merged into the beginnings of a coherent theology. Liberation theologians argued God was on the side of the poor in the Bible. As God worked in history, God was on the side of the poor now. There was injustice in this world, causing poverty in all its forms; this injustice was sinful. Yet, salvation through liberation would bring about justice in God's new heaven and new earth.

---

46 'Not only is the growth of the Kingdom not reduced to temporal progress; because of the Word accepted in faith, we see that the fundamental obstacle to the Kingdom, which is sin, is also the root of all misery and injustice; we see that the very meaning of the growth of the Kingdom is also the ultimate precondition for a just society and a new man' (Gutiérrez, 1974, p. 176). The spiritual realm is not rejected.

47 It continues to be the case today as we see in the example of CEAS.

## Context in the North

The emergence of liberation theology caused a spectrum of reactions in the North. It emerged directly alongside the calls for a theology of development in the WCC discussions. In fact, liberation theologians, drawing on their experiences in base communities, provided answers to many of the questions the WCC theologians posed. So how would the North react?

In response to the emergence of liberation theology, this theology of development faded into the background. Many WCC theologians (North and South) took forward themes in liberation. They preferred to use the terminology of liberation and justice rather than development.

From the opposite end of the spectrum, there was a rejection of the theology of liberation and in its place arose a prosperity theology, a defence of capitalism. For example, Michael Novak, an American Catholic theologian, countered liberation theology with his understanding of the congruity of Christianity with the capitalist system. Michel Camdessus, head of the IMF, adopted a similar theological stance but went further, co-opting the language of the 'bias toward the poor'. He argued that this theology was good for the poor. A spectrum of economic theology emerged that might critique aspects of capitalism but accepted the paradigm as a whole and the move toward 'globalization' in place of development. In fact, the North once again did not begin with the poor, they began with the rich and assumed the policies that were good for the rich were good for the poor.

## Conclusion

This chapter started with the Latin American elite promoting industrialization with the Catholic Church on their side. It ends with many bishops, priests, and parishioners having moved to the side of the poor, critiquing development and calling for a search for alternatives. From this call emerged the theology of liberation.

The following chapter explores the reaction of the North to the rejection of development and the call for liberation. In contrast to the confusion in the North, liberation theology emerged consistently from communities and theologians such as Gutiérrez. The question was whether Northern theologians would move toward liberation or try to reconcile the division between theology and development policies.

A theology of development asked if development was salvation. Liberation theology answered, liberation is salvation. A theology of development asked if there was a need to reduce the wealth of the rich; liberation theology answered yes. A theology of development asked what the new heaven and the new earth meant for practice in the here and now; liberation theology answered 'aim for justice'. And finally, a theology of development asked if humanity should be at the centre and liberation theology said yes, at the centre of liberation.

Would theologians in the North continue to call for development in the face of theological confusion? Or would they begin to follow a theology of liberation as their themes suggested?

# Part II

## *Changes*

# 3

# A Theology of Development:
# Stagnation and Disappearance

## Introduction

Our discussion of the changes from 1970 to 2000 in some ways bridges the divide between North and South, although the North remained prioritized. Development and its effects were argued about by people in the North and South. And, after the end of the Cold War, the focus on 'globalization' subsumed development, again encompassing both North and South. See Figure 5.

| 1950s–1980s | Economic Development (Capitalism) | Liberation from: Development For: ? |
|---|---|---|
| 1990s–Today | Globalization (Capitalism) | Liberation from: Globalization For: ? |

Figure 5

Theologians stopped discussing development. There was no 'theology of development', even though faith-based development agencies continued to work through development themes. Instead, the discussion diverged. Some northern theologians turned toward themes in liberation, as the following chapter explores. Others moved in the opposite direction. The counterpoint to liberation theology became not a theology of development but a theology of the free market and of prosperity.[1] The focus remained on the economic realm and the lines became drawn between support for capitalism and rejection of capitalism, again assuming an East–West divide. Since our controversy is between a 'theology of development' and a 'theology of liberation', I will introduce the counters of this capitalist theology briefly, to show the spread of the arguments. See Figure 6.

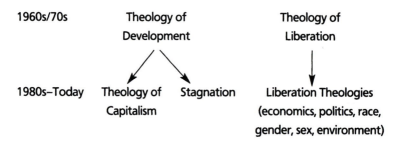

Figure 6

Thus, after discussing the changes in development practice, we will consider the following questions. What shifts occur in the debate over a theology of development in the North? What questions emerge in the new delineation? How did the South react to these changes?

## Changing development practice[2]

In the 1970s, northern development practice focused on lending money to poorer countries for large-scale development projects. The North

---

1 No theology encouraged development; it was either rejected or capitalism was supported. There was no theological project like liberation theology. The WCC project related to themes in liberation over time. Instead, theologians suggested theology could support the status quo: neoliberal capitalism. A theology of capitalism became a theology of development without being explicit and the narrowing of the definition of development to economic growth seemed justified. In fact, the focus of this theology was the North.

2 I cannot detail 30 years of changes in this book. However, I've highlighted

assumed developing countries needed aid to achieve economic growth. This situation led to a debt crisis in the 1980s and then a period of 'structural adjustment' in poorer countries. In the past 15 years, the conversation in the economic realm has shifted from development[3] to 'globalization'.[4] International trade has increased exponentially and has become central to development or globalization practice.

In the 1960s and 70s, although some theorists and practitioners in countries in the South argued that development was failing, the focus of the countries in the North remained on the economic realm. They wanted to ensure countries in the South continued to pursue capitalist development policies.[5] Aid was directed from the North to the South. Private banks, country governments, the IMF and the World Bank loaned money to southern governments for large-scale development projects. The banks wanted to lend as much as possible because they had

---

some of the points that moved us to where we are in the field today. There are several footnotes that detail where you can find further information on any of the theory and practice mentioned here.

3 This coincided with what was called 'an impasse in development studies'. See development theorist, Frans Schuurman's *Beyond the Impasse*. Since then, much work has been done in the field of development studies but the 'global' conversation has changed to one of 'globalization'. In development studies, there has been a move toward post-development, and a focus on alternatives. See, for example, Sachs, *The Development Dictionary*, Rahnema and Bawtree, *The Post-development Reader* and Kothari, *A Radical History of Development Studies*.

4 The verb 'to globalize' means 'to make global' or 'to make worldwide in scope of application' (www.m-w.com). Globalization is a noun, which means the making global of something. It is commonly used alone, which hides what it is that is being made global. If used properly, it would be linked with the word 'of'. Globalization, in this case, usually meant the globalization of capitalism, but I specify different definitions as the chapters continue.

5 Politics were subsumed under economics. As Latin American governments moved away from capitalist development policies, the USA and some European nations supported military takeovers. The previous chapter provided the example of Brazil. Democracy was replaced by military dictatorship in the interest of national security.

large amounts of money being deposited from oil rich countries.[6] Consequently, during the 1970s, countries across Latin America and Africa became heavily indebted to these northern countries and banks. At the same time, the large-scale development projects funded by these loans failed to bring about sustained economic growth and poverty reduction.

In the early 1980s, the situation worsened as the northern countries fell into a recession. Inflation rose and interest on the debt repayments skyrocketed. Southern countries could not repay the debts but could not declare bankruptcy. By 1982, there was a crisis. To continue the loan repayments, new loans were needed. These new loans enabled the South to repay the interest on the older loans. However, they were then saddled with new loans they could not pay. A vicious spiral began that continues today.

To counter the 'growth failure',[7] the IMF and the World Bank[8] made these new loans conditional on a process of 'structural adjustment'.[9] The banks argued that the southern countries failed to implement policies to encourage growth. They needed to adjust their structures, including reducing expenditures on health care, education and other social support areas, to focus on generating foreign (US and European) currency to pay the debts. They had to emphasize exports to US and European markets.[10] International trade became the main focus of development.

The emphasis on capitalism was narrowed to 'neoliberal' capitalism. Both British Prime Minister Margaret Thatcher (1979–90) and US

---

6 OPEC (Organization of Petroleum Exporting Countries) countries deposited their profits in American, British or European banks. The banks needed to find borrowers for this money and so they turned to poor countries.

7 This was the failure to sustain economic growth (to repay debts and to develop).

8 The private banks no longer wanted to lend to countries in such a risky situation. The IMF and the World Bank remained the only option for poorer countries.

9 For further details of this process, see Mosley, 1991.

10 Latin American development practitioners had rejected this focus back in the 1950s. They were forced to take it up again.

President Ronald Reagan (1981–89) pushed forward the idea that the free market was the key to economic growth. Development policies had failed because the markets were not free enough. Economists and politicians began to argue that wealth had to increase in the North too, to have a trickle-down effect on the South. The North had to generate enough money to buy the exports of the South to give the South the foreign currency it needed to repay the debtor.[11] In this view, there was a moving column of history, which followed a straight line toward development. The back of the column suffered along the way but that was a price that had to be paid.[12]

The role for the state also changed. Dictatorships, with their careful management of the development process, were replaced by democratic governments, which would leave the economic realm alone. As the state had led the large-scale projects and failed, development was turned over to the private sector and to CSOs.

Throughout the 1990s, the neoliberal perspective remained but the terminology changed from 'development' to 'globalization'. The Cold War had ended; it appeared the West had won as the East opened their markets to democratic capitalism. Now, the West/North argued, all countries should conform to the capitalist economic model; there was no alternative.[13] Globalization proponents argued that the capitalist system with free trade would achieve development.[14]

---

11 Loan repayments made the North wealthier. In the short term, a loan allowed a southern country to have money for a project. In the long term, the North received billions of dollars in interest, in addition to its original money back. So there has consistently been a net transfer of money from the South to the North.

12 Debt repayments are an example of this. An even more dramatic example would be of a hedge fund that buys poor country debts. The fund can buy debt from a bank or government at a discount and then act as a debt collection agency. The debt cannot be cancelled as countries cannot go bankrupt. See, for example, the case of Peru. A hedge fund bought part of its debt at a discounted $11 million and won a court case forcing it to repay a total of $58 million. See http://www.jubileeresearch.org/jubilee2000/news/vulture141000.html.

13 Thatcher is famous for this saying.

14 For example, DfID argued that globalization benefited the poor when governments were effective and markets were efficient. It trusted the private sector

And so, the centre of development became international trade. In 1995, the WTO began to govern international trade. Neoliberal capitalist theories argued that trade must be free. However, the rich countries continued to protect their own economies.[15]

While the WTO became the place where the rules on international trade were agreed, it was not the only international organization to enforce the rules. The World Bank and the IMF continued to impose conditions on their loans and grants, which required these countries to follow WTO rules. The World Bank's 2001 World Development Report continued to call for economic growth with poverty reduction through the market. 'Traditional elements of strategies to foster economic growth – macroeconomic stability and market-friendly reforms – are essential for

---

to trade in the interests of the poor, through self-regulation. DfID argued that inequality was lessening and would continue to lessen as the process of globalization continued (UKDfID).

15 The clearest examples come from the USA and the EU, which have protected their own economic sectors while trying to open those of other countries. For example, at the time of publishing, Canada, along with other countries, was in the process of making a complaint to the WTO about US corn subsidies. In theory, each country participating in the WTO has one vote in the decision-making process. However, in practice, not all countries can exercise their vote equally. Some countries in the global South have only one WTO delegate, responsible for the approximately 1,000 meetings that occur in the WTO each year. The subjects dealt with range from agriculture through air transport legislation to the definition of a particular tariff. Not only does the representative need to understand every topic but s/he is also to influence decision-making to the benefit of the home country. In contrast, the USA and EU each have several WTO delegates. And, they fly in experts to participate in sessions and advise their delegates at every stage. These experts can be from the companies that benefit from the rulings. Recent phases of trade talks suggest that some southern countries are trying to work together to demand certain changes. A group of 21 countries caused an impasse at a 2003 meeting in Mexico because they refused to make any changes before the USA and the EU changed their own trading restrictions. Yet, the majority of poorer countries still argue the rules are not fair. For example, see Aileen Kwa's article *Power Politics in the WTO*, for developing country delegate interviews, http://www.focusweb.org/publications/Books/power-politics-in-the-WTO.pdf

reducing poverty'[16] (World Bank, 2001, vi). More and more aspects of daily life were allocated to the private sector.

Further, the majority of international trade is between transnational companies[17] not between states or individuals. Although supported in the free market model, these TNCs can have negative impacts on the poor and on the local areas where aspects of their business were located. For example, at a local level, a TNC may invest in an area because wages are low and benefits do not exist. In addition, TNCs can invest in violent and/or undemocratic government regimes ensuring their survival.[18] These negative effects occur because TNCs are accountable to their investors not to local residents.[19] Proponents argue that the benefits, stimulating economic growth, outweigh these negative impacts.

During this time period, in alternative development theories and in many CSOs, there was a shift from large-scale development projects to small-scale development projects, emphasizing sustainability and participation.[20] However, the shift toward development as a private and civil sector matter allowed the nations in the North to ignore the shifting discourse. They promoted the free market and the western brand of democracy. Calls for alternatives to the dominant discourse and practice also emerged, as we'll see in the following chapters.[21] Yet, these small-

---

16 This document and its focus on poverty caused many arguments within the World Bank between those who put free markets above all else and those who were more qualified in their approval. See Wade, 2001.

17 I use 'transnational' rather than 'multinational' to emphasize that, although the company may be 'based' in a particular country, it does not necessarily follow the laws of that country. They often operate outside any national entity.

18 They can violate human rights. For example, people who have protested against the entrance of TNCs have been killed. Perhaps the most famous case is that of Ken Saro-Wiwa, author and activist, executed in Nigeria, after protesting for years against petroleum companies.

19 See Richter, 2001 for details of problems and suggested solutions. We will see this critique arise again in the case of Christian Aid. See Curtis, 2001.

20 For example, see Redclift, *Sustainable Development*; Chambers, *Rural Development: Putting the Last First* & *Whose Reality Counts? Putting the First Last*, and again Kothari, *A Radical History of Development Studies*.

21 These can be blended with themes in liberation.

scale efforts were dwarfed by the forcefulness and scale of the push for economic globalization.

## A fading theology of development

In the face of this shifting practice, what happened to the theology of development? It stagnated. Instead, theologies moved forward considering the economy from the perspective of the capitalist free market and globalization, and oppositely, from the perspective of ending capitalism. Development did not receive overt theological support. This split, in a way, followed the move of global development practice itself in the 1980s and early 1990s.[22] There was no theological analysis of the development practice that increased loans to poorer countries or that focused on large-scale projects or that promoted structural adjustment.[23]

While the Catholic Church and the WCC continued to discuss issues of justice, the word 'development' moved into the background and the call for a 'theology of development' seemed to disappear.[24] Justice, participation and sustainability became foci.[25] WCC documents reflect this trend too. For example, the WCC through the Commission on the Churches' Participation on Development published a trilogy on 'The

---

22 Rather than working to ensure that economic growth achieved poverty reduction, proponents of development assumed that poverty would be reduced by growth. There was no alternative. Now that the shift is toward 'globalization', theologies are emerging that overtly support aspects of globalization. See, for example, the series *God and Globalization*, edited by Max L. Stackhouse and others.

23 Alternatively, we did see theologians dealing with relieving the debts of the world's poorest countries as a result of the debt crisis, as the next chapter explores briefly. Rather than being a theology of development, calls for debt relief were countering the harmful effects of development using themes emerging from liberation.

24 SODEPAX ended its work in 1980.

25 In 1975, at Nairobi, the WCC began to call for a 'just, participatory and sustainable society'. Then, in 1983, the language shifted to a new programme for 'Justice, Peace and the Integrity of Creation' (JPIC).

Church and the Poor', which ends with this statement: 'we propose that the churches reconsider their organized structures to permit maximum deployment of their resources to the struggles for a just, participatory, liberated and sustainable society' (Santa Ana, 1979, p. 202).[26] In place of development, the theme of liberation emerged.[27]

As the global focus remained on the Cold War, however, there was also concern about nuclear proliferation and the possibility of nuclear war. In 1979, the WCC conference focused on Faith, Science and the Future.[28] Here, the environment and sustainability came into focus. The Chernobyl disaster in 1986, among other examples, showed clearly the links between the nuclear proliferation and the destruction of the environment. Here, again, the focus seemed to be the East–West conflict.

There was a clear move away from the word 'development' to larger themes, encompassing questions of 'justice', nuclear technology and war, and the environment. This reflected the divide between development and liberation that the WCC was trying to bridge. It seems it was not possible to continue 'developing' a theology of development in the face of a clear liberation theology.[29]

---

26  This trilogy included *Good News to the Poor: The Challenge of the Poor in the History of the Church; Separation Without Hope?: Essays on the Relation between the Church and the Poor During the Industrial Revolution and Western Colonial Expansion*, and *Towards a Church of the Poor: The Work of an Ecumenical Group on the Church and the Poor*.

27  Some theologians, including many associated with the WCC, took on board liberation concepts and continued to work with them, condemning capitalism and searching for alternatives. For example, we will see Gutiérrez, Uruguayan theologian Julio de Santa Ana, and German theologian Ulrich Duchrow, among others in the following chapter.

28  See, for example, Abrecht and Francis, eds, *Facing up to Nuclear Power* (1975) and Abrecht and Koshy, eds, *Before It's Too Late* (1984).

29  As the WCC moved away from representing ideas emerging from the North, it has been seen to lose influence. Yet, it deliberately tries to work from a more global perspective. It would be interesting to examine if this assumption of the loss of 'power' of the WCC was actually a loss of influence of the USA and Europe therein.

Those within the Catholic Church also moved to both sides of the spectrum, away from development. Pope Paul VI seemed to be supportive of the emerging liberation theology, in light of Vatican II and Latin American developments.[30] In 1978, John Paul II became Pope. After this, the Vatican pulled back from, and then later condemned, aspects of liberation theology. It neither wholeheartedly supported nor rejected capitalism but it, too, did not continue to discuss development. However, on both sides of the debate, Catholic theologians strayed from the Vatican line.[31] Novak, for example, argued for a theology of capitalism and, within capitalism, of the free market.

In summary, there was still no clear Christian basis for development practice emerging. Instead, economic theologies emerged supporting the narrowing of development to economic growth without being explicit. These theologies of capitalism were at first seen to be on the margins themselves. The churches, development agencies and WCC seemed to be taking on board the discussions from within liberation theology.[32] However, by the mid-1980s through the 1990s, these economic theologies became prominent, as the secular neoliberal policies did too.[33] The first shift from a theology of development to one of liberation, shifted again. The global Christian conversation turned to support

---

30  See Dussel, 1981 and 1992 for details of further interaction between Latin American liberation theology and the Vatican during the 1970s.

31  For example, US Catholic Bishops produced *Economic Justice for All*, critiquing the American economy. And the next chapter continues to consider Catholic liberation theologians.

32  For example, see Elliott's *Comfortable Compassion?*. Elliott was director of Christian Aid 1983-4.

33  For example, the volume *On Moral Business* (Stackhouse *et al.*, 1995) contained a section on 'the call for new Christian paradigms'. One 1981 article by Robert Benne, Lutheran ethicist, argued that he felt sidelined as he called for a theology supportive of capitalism. A 1990 article published by Amy Sherman detailed the shift in thinking over those ten years. For Sherman, since socialism had been proven wrong, it was time for the free market policies and their supporting theology to take centre stage and for churches to acknowledge this shift. The shift from 'development' to a focus on the capitalist marketplace was almost complete.

of capitalism.[34] And, with the end of the Cold War, rather than moving to consider the North–South divide, the conversation turned to 'globalization'.

## A theology of capitalism and consumption?

In the call for a theology of development, several questions around theology and development emerged but were not answered. Liberation theology answered the questions in one way. An emerging theology supportive of capitalism provided different answers. A theology of development did not continue. For example, the question 'Is development salvation?' disappeared. There was no discussion of development as salvation. Instead, the focus narrowed to how capitalism was 'Christian'.[35] 'Is it possible that, in face of the new evidence (the end of the Cold War), everyone who holds to a "preferential option for the poor" must now embrace capitalism . . .? In some measure, the answer is Yes' (Stackhouse and McCann et al., 1995, p. 950). Within this capitalist theology, there was further discussion of riches, the new heaven and new earth, and humanity. These 'economic theologies' became a counter-

---

34 This shift remained as we moved into the era of 'globalization' and now the question is whether the calls for alternatives and liberation theologies will once again become prominent or whether the theological support for capitalism will continue. What is certain is that the calls for a theology of development still have not been answered. Toward the end of this period, we can see the beginnings of the word 'development' popping up again in this capitalist theology. For example, Sherman's 1997 book *The Soul of Development: Biblical Christianity and Economic Transformation in Guatemala* equated development with 'democratic capitalism'. While there was not an explicit theology of development present, there was both an implicit and explicit assumption that Christianity could and did support capitalism. An even more dramatic example is Camdessus. He uses the exact language of liberation theology and assumes neoliberal capitalism, alongside IMF policies, is that liberation. See Camdessus as quoted in Hinkelammert 1997.

35 Not all these theologians agreed with each other as to how 'Christian' capitalism was and to what extent its effects could and should be mitigated. These theologians, however, do support the global capitalist system.

point to liberation theologies.[36] While they have been used to justify aspects of development in the global conversation, they were not a theology of development. In fact, they focused on the North, all but ignoring the South, justifying the wealth of the North and arguing that this wealth could be used wisely.

### What should the North do with its riches?

A theology of development had raised three questions with regard to riches. How much wealth should the North have? How should the wealthy use their riches? What is the relationship between the worship of wealth and the worship of God? By the 1980s, alongside neoliberal policies, the focus turned to the second question.[37] Countering liberation theology, the accumulation of wealth was assumed to be positive. These theologians argued the North should use its riches in two ways: 1. To consume; 2. To steward.

> Almighty God did not make creation coercive, but designed it in an arena of liberty. Within that arena, God has called for individuals and peoples to live according to His law and inspiration. Democratic capitalism has been designed to permit them, sinners all, to follow this free pattern. It creates a noncoercive society as an arena of liberty, within which individuals and peoples are called to realize, through democratic methods, the vocations to which they believe they are called. (Novak, 1982, pp. 359–60)

Basing his theology on the individual, Novak celebrated the market as a positive mechanism through which Christians could act.[38] This theo-

---

36 I am only providing a small sample of economic theology here. There is a far more extensive list of theologians and economists working in the areas of theology and economics, for example: Alasdair MacIntyre, Stanley Hauerwas, Stephen Long and Bob Goudzwaard. These theologians vary in their assessment of capitalism.

37 The other two questions both find prominent places in liberation theologies, as seen in the following chapter.

38 He deliberately counters liberation theology in his work *Will It Liberate?*

logy prioritized competition between individuals rather than co-operation in community. 'To compete . . . is not a vice. It is, in a sense, the form of every virtue and an indispensable element in natural and spiritual growth. Competition is the natural play of the free person' (Novak, 1982, p. 347). The three foci of capitalism (the individual, profit, and growth) were all supported. This theology also supported the theory that wealth should trickle down from the richest to the poorest and the neoliberal theory of a market, free from government interference.

Others accepted the need to mitigate poverty, but not to the detriment of the wealthy. Harries, for example, argued that Christians should work to counter poverty.[39] However, this needed to occur in the global capitalist economy, which was 'underpinned by Christian values' because it is 'the worst system we've got – except for all the others' (Harries, 1992, p. 11). For Harries, there was no alternative but to take care of the poor in this system.

These theologians did not see the poor as the starting point for theology. 'There is only one Gospel, for rich and poor alike' (Harries, 1992, p. 165). The existence of a gap between the rich and the poor was not seen as the centre of injustice, of sin. This theology focused on the wealthy.

So, assuming the wealthy should have their riches, how should they use them? First, consumption became a focus.[40] 'Identity in today's society . . . is no longer given by ethnicity, class, gender or social status. People find out who they are or who they want to be, by consumption' (Sedgwick, 1999, p. 109).[41] Capitalism assumes that human beings were

---

39 Richard Harries is an Anglican bishop, addressing his words to those who are rich. His book was entitled *Is There a Gospel for the Rich? Christian Obedience in a Capitalist World.*

40 We see this in the case of Christian Aid too.

41 Sedgwick is interpreting Jean Baudrillard. Peter Sedgwick is a British theologian and lecturer, working in theology and economies. Like Harries, Sedgwick addressed his words to the rich. Rather than arguing that capitalism and a focus on the market denied human identity, he wanted to find a place for human identity therein. While Sedgwick was more circumspect about his approval of the capitalist system than Novak, he still argued that 'alongside the poverty and

natural consumers. Accepting this, some theologians argued that consumerism would not disappear, so its effects should be modified. 'We
need to find a new context for consumerism, which preserves the
concern for identity and relationships, but puts them in a transformed
reality of transcendence, wider social relationships and services of others
as well as self' (Sedgwick, 1999, p. 138). People needed to be able to
counter the impersonal accumulation advocated by the global economy.
Three area of focus were suggested here: ethical consumption, reducing
consumption, and the question of debt.[42] Again, the initial focus seemed
to be on the individual, rather than on structures, and on the North rather
than the South.

Second, the question of stewardship arose.[43] 'Creation, ownership,
and stewardship' were emphasized (Finn, 1996, p. 47). For Finn,[44] the
world was created by God and given to humans, to be owned. 'The
giftedness of the world implies a relation of intentionality between God
and the earth's inhabitants' (p. 49). As humans owned the earth, they
should 'steward' it, take care of it. Christians in the North might steward
more resources (including money) than Christians in the South; that
was fine. 'Those who have money are obliged by it to become careful
stewards, under pain of losing it or cutting foolishly into their capital'

---

exploitation there are also the great benefits provided by the next stage of global
capitalism' (Sedgwick, 1999, pp. 272-3). His and Harries' are pragmatic arguments. They do not speak to those excluded from the global economy and so
marginalize the poorest further.

42 With ethical consumption and reducing consumption comes a question, not
of decreasing wealth, but using wealth wisely. The aspect of not having the right
to wealth disappeared. The question of debt is taken up briefly in the following
chapter in the context of a fuller critique of wealth.

43 Again, although stewardship is mentioned as in the call for a theology of
development, it was not discussed specifically in relation to development or to a
theology of development. Where it was discussed in relation to poverty, it seemed
to merge with themes in liberation theology. See, for example, Ronald Sider's 'A
Biblical Perspective on Stewardship', in Stackhouse *et al.*, eds, 1995, *On Moral
Business*.

44 Daniel Finn is an American professor of economics and theology.

(Novak, 1982, p. 348). For Novak, Christians who owned the resources should ensure that they were used as God intended.

What, then, could be said about the second set of questions that arose in the call for a theology of development?

### *What did the new heaven and the new earth mean for economic and political structures?*

According to these theologians, the global capitalist system was not sinful, although some argued that its effects should be tempered. 'Democratic capitalism is by no means the Kingdom of God' (Novak, 1982, p. 338). However, its characteristics were Christian and the capitalist system could point toward God's kingdom. 'If the Kingdom of God were here in its fullness, we could happily give away everything that we possess and trust moment-by-moment for God to provide' (Harries, 1992, p. 48). However, God's kingdom had not arrived and so not only was the global capitalist system acceptable, self-interest was acceptable too.

Moving even further toward the notion of capitalism as a Christian economy, Novak argued for a theology of the TNC. 'Such a theology should attempt to show how corporations may be instruments of redemption, of human purposes and values, of God's grace' (Novak, 1995, p. 784). Corporations could have Christian values and could point toward God's kingdom.

Work is now being done again on structures with regard to principalities and powers in the context of globalization.[45] Max Stackhouse, a professor of Christian ethics, described several principalities and powers, including Mammon: that which governs 'a viable economy in order to provide the food, shelter, clothing and opportunity for work and property for people to survive'; and Mars: the political 'system of gaining, legitimating and using coercive authority to control violence' (Stackhouse,

---

45 Stackhouse has edited three volumes of *God and Globalization: 1. Religion and the Powers of the Common Life*, 2. *The Spirit and the Modern Authorities*, and 3. *Christ and the Dominions of Civilization.*

2000, p. 37). He also, however, began with support for globalization. As the introduction to the series asked, 'What are the ways that religion, theology, and ethics, in close interaction with our social, political, and economic situation can help guide globalization?' (iii). Globalization is something to be accepted and managed, as capitalism was.

So what did this mean for practice? There is a spectrum of calls for hands off and hands on management of the global capitalist system but the primary focus remained on the individual.

## Should humanity be at the centre of development?

Although this specific question was not answered, the focus narrowed within capitalism to the individual. Novak argued that the capitalist system was just, prioritizing the freedom of individuals over justice in community. Through participation in the market, he argued, those individuals who work hard received the reward of money and those who did not received their just reward of poverty. As Finn argued, those who are wealthier did not need to give up riches, but use them for God's purpose.

The theologians reconceptualized justice,[46] in light of the acceptance of the global capitalist system. For Stackhouse, because there was not an alternative to globalization, justice had to be dealt with within this context. Harries too reconfigured the notion of justice in this world. 'In the light of a Christian and human understanding, there is justice when neither partner in a relationship is in a position either to exploit or patronize the other; when they meet on a basis of equality' (Harries, 1992, p. 57). Harries' definition of the global economy, in contrast, was one of power inequality. 'It will always reflect the interest of the most powerful and work to their advantage against the most vulnerable' (p. 94). Instead of rejecting the capitalist system, however, he suggested reform, because 'there is a basic congruity between the Christian faith and the free market' (pp. 3–4). For Harries, the global capitalist system, although unjust, did not conflict with Christianity.

---

46 There was no emphasis on injustice. Further, where the WCC moved from development to justice because the two seemed incompatible, these theologians reconfigured justice within the global capitalist system.

## Context in the South

While liberation theologies emerged in the face of a push for development, they had to be formalized in a world that pushed for global capitalism at all costs. They no longer had to counter a theology of development but a theology that supported capitalism. Those previously involved in a discussion of development in the North moved toward justice, and away from talk of development.[47]

Yet, again theologians in the South were forced to respond to the categories put in place by the North. When they began to discuss a third way, they were labelled as communist. During the 1970s and 80s, they remained shoehorned into the East–West struggle. After the fall of the Berlin Wall, they were sidelined altogether, presumed dead along with socialism. A capitalist theology was quite happy to discuss the wealth of the North and how it should be used, beginning theology with the rich and ignoring the poor.

However, liberation theologies were springing up around the world. Latin Americans were also joined by northern theologians like Ulrich Duchrow, Anglican theologian and professor Timothy Gorringe, and Catholic theologian Mary Grey who dealt with liberation themes including ecology and feminism. As North American, Asian, African, black, feminist, and ecological theologies of liberation emerged, the themes within liberation also expanded from the economic realm. Still encompassing economic alternatives, these theologies began to consider themes of race, gender, environment, sex and politics. So what did liberation theologies have to offer the global conversation that no longer argued between development and liberation?

---

47 Elliott and others draw on liberation themes. We will see the same is true of Christian Aid now, perhaps still reflecting the tradition of his directorship. Michael Taylor, another Christian Aid director in the 1990s also mirrors this discussion.

## Conclusion

The emerging theology of development found nowhere to go. The powerful policy-makers in the North ignored liberation theology and continued with international development practice that increased the riches of the North. Economic theologies developed that supported this increase in wealth. They also supported the move toward 'globalization' after the end of the Cold War. Rather than facing the gap between critical theology and development policy, a theology developed that moved outside of 'development' altogether, focused on the free market and the push for capitalism. Christianity seemed to support acquiring wealth, consumption and stewardship. Aspects of liberation theology were both condemned and co-opted by the North; for example, a redefining of justice.

However, within development studies itself, alternatives had been emerging. What did development practitioners do in the face of this extreme theology? Could it be that a theology of liberation offered a better alternative for development practitioners than the global capitalist theology?

# 4

# Theologies of Liberation: Expansion and Formalization

## Introduction

Our discussion of changes in liberation also bridges the divide between the North and the South. From the 1970s, liberation theologies flourished in regions around the world. Some northern theologians began to engage with the themes of liberation, rather than continuing a conversation over a theology of development. The conversation was no longer solely about eradicating one's own poverty, but richer/powerful people began to consider the need to reduce their wealth/power. Beginning with one's own experience remained, recognizing that the goal is to move from injustice toward justice. In this chapter, we explore the alternatives to development and globalization along with the theologies of liberation.

Liberation theologians in the North and South continued to deal with economics and politics and began to include themes of race, gender, sex, environment, etc. Not only were the wealthy prioritized over the poor but the economic realm itself was prioritized, white was prioritized, male was prioritized, heterosexuality was prioritized, etc. They asked what these various expressions of poverty had to say about Christianity and what Christianity had to say about these forms of poverty.

As liberation theology was formalized, particularly in Latin America, some theologians moved away from the roots of the method: the hermeneutical circle in communities of the poorest. As theologians responded to criticisms from policymakers and other theologians, they began to systematize, instead of continuing to reflect the voices of people

87

on the ground.[1] These liberation theologians were themselves challenged by a new generation of voices to reflect on their own forms of oppression.[2] And so liberation theologies both formalized and expanded in themes.

After discussing the changes in liberation and alternatives to development and globalization, we will consider the following questions. What shifts occur in the debate over a theology of liberation? What questions emerge in the new delineation? Where does that leave the situation today?

## Liberation practice:[3] political and economic alternatives[4]

During the 1960s through 80s, governments in the North supported various Latin American military dictatorships. These dictatorships carried out severe political repression. Anyone who opposed the government or its policies was subject to investigation. Thousands of people

---

1 Today, liberation theology needs to return to these roots, to the voices on the ground that reflect theologically on their own situations of injustice, as the final chapter will argue. Some of this work is already beginning. See Petrella's *Latin American Liberation Theology: The Next Generation* and *The Future of Liberation Theology*. See also Ottmann's *Lost for Words?* and Burdick's *Legacies of Liberation* for further case studies.

2 There is not space to fully trace this shift. I refer to various liberation theologies throughout the chapter and have further suggested readings in several footnotes.

3 Within the field of development studies, the focus on small-scale projects, participation, self-determination, and non-economic factors does not seem to have changed the macro-level practice. Many of the small-scale moves in development were toward liberation while the large-scale moves continued to ignore or co-opt the language of liberation to meet the goals of 'globalization'.

4 Again, my examples come from Latin America, and Brazil in particular, and are mainly limited to the economic and political realms due to lack of space. However, even within Latin America, the theologies expanded, considering themes of power in race, gender, etc. See, for example, Batstone *et al.*, 1997, *Liberation Theologies, Postmodernity, and the Americas*.

were murdered and 'disappeared' in countries across Latin America.[5] Perhaps the example most well-known internationally is that of El Salvadoran Archbishop Oscar Romero.[6]

In Brazil, the coup was both to deter the masses from turning to socialism and to boost the stagnant economy.[7] However, there was an economic recession in the late 1970s and early 1980s. The elite in Brazil, wealthy businesspeople, wanted a change and in discussion with the military leaders moved from dictatorship to democracy.[8] The struggle by communities on the ground was ignored. The call for direct elections by the masses was ignored. Instead, the wealthy voices were heard and democracy was reintroduced by a minority in 1984.[9] The majority of Brazilians remained excluded from political decision-making.[10]

Perhaps, as dictatorships could change to democracy,[11] capitalism could change to another economic system. Yet, according to the North, capitalism and democracy now had to go together. Some theorists and practitioners became frustrated with the focus on capitalist economics, even in the political realm. In a capitalist democracy, the state seemed to exist to promote capitalism, to ensure the working of the market.[12]

---

5 See Dussel, for example, for further details. This situation has still not been resolved in the minds of many Latin Americans, as the political leaders have not been brought to justice for these crimes.

6 In fact, his move toward liberation was stimulated in part by the murder of an El Salvadoran priest Rutilio Grande.

7 See Eakin, 1997.

8 They were following northern arguments.

9 It had been uprooted by a minority in the first place.

10 Brazilian critics argue that each new wave of political leadership has been co-opted into the policies and corruption of the old. See, for example, the cases of Fernando Henrique Cardoso, sociologist and former dependency theorist and now 'Lula', Luiz Inácio da Silva, born into poverty and a former trade unionist. Goertzl, 1994 analyzes Cardoso's presidency. See newspaper articles for the most recent comments on Lula's presidency.

11 Remember that these dictatorships were not satisfactorily accomplishing economic growth in their countries. Northern governments argued that perhaps a more democratic rule, with government not interfering in the marketplace, would achieve economic growth.

12 See Nandy 1992 for an analysis of the role of the state in development.

Capitalism shifted power from participating in the government to participating in the economic realm. Citizens depended on the marketplace and on TNCs rather than on their democratic governments. In countries like Brazil, the shift from dictatorship to democracy was less effective, as citizens still had to have money to make their voices heard in the marketplace. And the poor remained excluded.[13]

In Brazil, for example, the elites continued to control politics, as they controlled the economy. People relied on the traditional system of patronage, by which individual politicians reward those personally who vote them into power.[14] The economic elite has remained stable through each political change, from colonialism through industrialization and development through military dictatorship and now through a capitalist democracy promoting 'globalization'.[15]

Yet, in Brazil, attempts have been made to make the government respond to its citizens. One example is the MST,[16] an organization that aims to redistribute uncultivated but productive land. Land distribution in Brazil is one of the most unequal in the world with less than 3 per cent of the population owning more than 60 per cent of the land that can be cultivated. The Brazilian Constitution made it illegal to own uncultivated land. In response, this landless movement began in 1985 when a group of landless took over an unused piece of land with the support of the

---

13 It would be interesting to analyse civil society in light of this discussion. CEAS begins this process in chapter 6. Critics have argued that in a liberal democracy, the emphasis is on receiving and enjoying rights, not on active participation. In this view, culture is relegated to civil society, as if it can be treated completely separately from economics and politics. This allows 'the global expansion of the western economy and the transformation of non-western societies into havens of western consumerism' (Sardar, 1998, p. 57). However, democracy and capitalism emerge from particular cultural backgrounds. Ziauddin Sardar is a Pakistani writer and cultural critic.

14 For further explanation of patronage, see Mainwaring, 1999.

15 Since Brazil's independence regional politicians have come from the wealthiest families. See Eakin, 1997.

16 *Movimento dos Trabalhadores Rurais sem Terra*, Rural Landless Workers' Movement. For those who read Portuguese, see www.mst.org for further details. For access to an English version of the website see www.mstbrazil.org.

Catholic Church. The workers formed a co-operative and later gained the official title to the land. The MST has more than 350,000 families who have gained ownership of small pieces of land.[17] This attempt at land reform harks back to the work of Brazilians in the early 1960s before the military coup. Not only is the goal to redistribute land but the land is then 'owned' by the co-operatives, not by an individual. It is a holistic alternative system to the global capitalist economy.[18]

Throughout the past 30 years,[19] many people in the South and North have been critical of development and dictatorship and have called for an end to development and for alternatives to globalization.[20] Returning to our definition of liberation, we begin with the call for *freedom from* development and globalization.

People calling for alternatives rejected four aspects of globalization. First, economy should not precede culture. The economy was assumed to be the basis of society.[21] This assumption allowed the expansion of one culture (western) and its economy (capitalism) across the globe, subsuming other cultures and economies.[22] Second, liberationists rejected the expansion of corporate power that came with the focus on the market.[23] Third, the expansion of finance and money exchange was rejected.[24]

---

17 Often, the landowners, although they have no constitutional right to the land, refuse to give it up, resulting in violence against the landless.

18 For further information on land reform and faith in Brazil, see Adriance's *Promised Land*.

19 I will not discuss all alternatives over the past 30 years. Rather, I'll summarize the situation as we moved into a new century.

20 Remember that globalization is defined as an expansion of capitalism.

21 This is true not only for capitalism but also for socialism and communism. Marx made this assumption too.

22 Thierry Verhelst, development practitioner, countered this assumption in *No Life Without Roots: Culture and Development*.

23 With the shift in emphasis to the private sector, TNCs had more economic power than most world governments and emphasized profit. See David Korten's *When Corporations Rule the World*. Korten is Founder of the People-Centered Development Forum.

24 International financial flows, for example, have grown to £2 trillion per day. See Singh, 2000 and, for a specific suggestion of how to harness these flows, see

Finally, exclusive ownership was rejected, in particular, biopiracy.[25] Patent law had been extended to cover natural resources and knowledge, which were previously considered common property.[26] Even nature, including genetic knowledge, could now be owned. Theologians and practitioners argued we needed freedom from this dominant economic ideology, from TNCs, from the domination of money, and from this exclusive ownership.

However, liberation is also *freedom to act*. So what action did liberationists call for?[27] We can begin here in the economic realm. What has often been ignored by the dominant discourse is the claim for heterogeneity over homogeneity. There were many suggested alternatives. Rather than the homogenous and hegemonic solution of capitalism, liberationists argued there could be heterogenous solutions. Thus, a

---

Patomaki 2001. In addition, one person, with access to money, could have more control over national economies than their own governments. See, for example, accounts by George Soros, critiquing his own market power.

25 In this view, the first phase of globalization began in the colonial period. Latin America and Africa were considered to be empty land waiting to be taken. The second phase of globalization extended the concept to people on the land. They were seen to be empty, needing to be owned or filled with Northern knowledge. Northern culture and knowledge was globalized. CEAS holds the same understanding of globalization.

26 For a detailed analysis of this piracy, see Shiva and Holla-Bhar, 1996. Vandana Shiva is a physicist, philosopher of science, and activist. Further, corporations have patented seed and are also using genome technology to keep seeds from germinating until a particular chemical is applied, forcing farmers to purchase further seed and materials every season.

27 Although I use many economic examples, liberation practice rejected the hegemony of this realm and moved to discussing politics, ecology, race, gender, and sex, for example. Central to the search for alternatives has been the rejection of a hegemonic system, as we saw with Camara. Liberationists did not want capitalism, socialism or communism as they had been implemented by the North. Yet, if they chose the capitalist option, they were under the hand of the USA and some of Europe. If they chose a socialist or communist option, they were rejected by the USA and were under the hand of the former USSR instead. One goal of liberation theology is no hegemonic system. Some alternatives listed here have socialist aspects. Others trace new ideas.

second focus has been on the local economic, political and cultural realms, again allowing the dominant discourse to ignore it. There is no 'one' alternative to globalization.

These new foci required new definitions. Economics, for example, would begin at the level of the family, at a local level and then expand out to larger communities.[28] 'Economics meant "the law or the management of the household"' (Meeks,[29] 1989, p. 3).[30] Economics was merged with a particular political and cultural context, as the term 'political economy' used to show. Political economy 'involves the social relationships of power among the members of a community in their attempt to earn a living' (Gorringe, 1994, p. 29).[31] The economic realm neither takes priority over other realms nor exists separately from other realms.

Perhaps even within economics growth should not be prioritized. One alternative argued that economies should aim for a steady state, developing an economy qualitatively rather than quantitatively.[32]

An economy in sustainable development adapts and improves in knowledge, organization, technical efficiency, and wisdom; it does this without assimilating or accreting an ever greater percentage of the

---

28  Some economists also criticize the basic tenets in use today. See Keen, 2001, for example.

29  M. Douglas Meeks is an American theologian who wrote, among other books, *God the Economist*.

30  Contrast this definition with the one in the *Penguin Dictionary of Economics*: 'the study of the production, distribution and consumption of wealth in human society' (p. 130).

31  Again, note the different definition in Bannock, Baxter and Davis, eds, 1992, *Penguin Dictionary of Economics*: 'an early title for the subject (economics), now sounds old-fashioned but usefully emphasizes the importance of choice between alternatives in economics which remains, despite continuing scientific progress, as much of an art as a science' (p. 130).

32  For further characteristics of a steady-state economy, see Daly, 1996 and Goodland, 1996. In another alternative, Colin Hines, Fellow of the International Forum on Globalization, advocated localization. Hines argued that some economic growth was possible but had to come only at the local level from savings and investment generated locally.

matter-energy of the ecosystem into itself but rather stops at a scale at which the remaining ecosystem can continue to function and renew itself year after year. (Daly, 1996, p. 195)

A steady-state economy recognizes ecological limits and works within these boundaries.[33]

Poverty would also be redefined. First, poverty could have a positive connotation in the economic realm. People overconsuming in the North need to become poorer. 'Poverty was . . . the name for a unique and ecologically sustainable style of coping with historically given, rather than technically construed, necessity, the "need" to face the unavoidable, not a lack' (Illich,[34] 1992, p. 93). One could choose to be economically poor but not be deprived of basic needs, living within ecological and other limits.

Second, poverty was not limited to the economic realm. Poverty was a lack of power with regard to any realm. It also merges realms, becomes an interdisciplinary concept. Consolidation of different types of power, economic, political, cultural, racial, sexual, etc., should not occur.[35] Take, for example, economic democracy:[36] 'democracy should not be considered as an electoral input over who controls the economy, but also in terms of access to participation in the economy and the development of individuals' and local communities' potential and capacities' (Hines,

---

33 Here we move beyond economics alone to consider communities holistically.

34 Ivan Illich was a development critic who worked for many years in Latin America.

35 International trade, for example, would be severely curtailed. TNCs are rejected. Amory Starr, sociologist, details how communities around the world are organizing to take apart TNCs. If a business is selling locally, then at least local citizens will have a means of controlling the business through their use of consumer power. This is called a site-here-to-sell-here rule (Hines, 2000, p. 63).

36 For an explanation of how economic democracy would affect the current system see Makhijani, 1992. Arjun Makhijani is an environmental scientist and president of the Institute for Energy and Environmental Research. Also see his 2004 *Manifesto for Global Democracy*.

2000, p. 118). People should be able to participate directly and fully in their communities, involved in more than deciding what to buy. These suggested changes focused on local communities holistically.[37]

## Formalizing and expanding liberation theologies

Throughout the 1970s and 1980s liberation theologies emerged from marginalized communities around the world, as different regions reflected from their own situations.[38] There are now theologies of liberation in North America, Africa, Asia, and Europe enveloping issues of race, gender, sex, class and environment.[39] In Latin America, they expanded out from Catholicism to Protestantism and to incorporate indigenous faiths. At the same time, liberation theologies were formalized and systematized. Issues important to communities in the North, such as Christology and soteriology have all been developed.

In the economic realm, liberation theologians began to engage more seriously with the economic discussions of socialism and Marxism, in their search for alternatives to the capitalist system.[40] At the beginning of

---

37 A healthy community would include: 'good housing, shops, and other facilities, with good public transport'; 'good education, training and work opportunities'; 'diverse wildlife and good air, water and soil quality'; 'low energy use and waste' and 'warm homes'; sustainable lifestyles with 'less unhealthy and unnecessary consumption and resource use'; 'a safe and healthy environment'; 'quality information enabling the monitoring of social, economic and environmental progress'; 'a vibrant and creative culture'; 'high levels of public participation in decision-making'; and finally, 'the means to facilitate on-going improvements in the area' (Korten, 1999, pp. 38–9).

38 Although most of my examples focus on economics to distinguish practice from the previous chapter, I refer to other realms in footnotes.

39 See for example: Kosuke Koyama, *No Handle on the Cross*; Aloysius Pieris, *An Asian Theology of Liberation*; Allan Boesak, *Farewell to Innocence*; James Cone, *A Black Theology of Liberation*, and Rosemary Ruether, *Gaia and God* and Commission on Theological Concerns of the Christian Conference of Asia, *Minjung Theology*.

40 See, for example, Miranda's *Marx and the Bible*.

liberation theology's engagement with the social sciences, theologians critiqued both capitalism and communism, searching for a third way. Forced to choose a side in the Cold War, they were not allowed to argue for a democracy based on something other than capitalism. In the midst of this struggle, many centred their work on socialist economic policies.

During the 1970s and 1980s, liberation theologians, priests and bishops were not only persecuted by their national governments, sometimes resulting in their deaths, but slowly they began to be rejected by the Roman Catholic Church itself. For example, during the 1980s, Cardinal Ratzinger, who is now Pope, encouraged the Vatican to investigate the Boff brothers and Gustavo Gutiérrez. Leonardo Boff was told by the Vatican to cease writing and lecturing.[41] Just previous to this occasion, the Vatican had issued an *Instruction on Certain Aspects of the 'Theology of Liberation'*, criticizing liberation theology.[42]

There were at least two aspects at issue. First, the Vatican wanted theologians to stop engaging with Marxist and communist theories; only capitalist theories were allowed.[43] From within the Latin American church hierarchy too, the trend began to appoint conservative bishops and priests into positions of power. This movement continued into the 1990s. Catholicism began to return to its prioritization of the elites, only now the language of liberation had been co-opted.

Second, Pope John Paul II was concerned that the theology of the Catholic Church emerge from the Pope, from the historical line reaching down from Peter. It should not spring up from the base of society, from

---

41 Boff's book *Church, Charism and Power: Liberation Theology and the Institutional Church* was published in Brazil in 1981. Cox's *The Silencing of Leonardo Boff: The Vatican and the Future of World Christianity* details these events.

42 For the full text, see the Vatican website: http://www.vatican.va/roman_curia/congregations/cfaith/documents/rc_con_cfaith_doc_19840806_theology-liberation_en.html

43 The Vatican rejected Marxism outright and although it did not reject capitalism, it did critique its excesses. Socialism falls between the two ends of this spectrum. Vatican pronouncements are interpreted differently depending on one's location.

BECs. The Vatican began to move back toward theological orthodoxy, promoting the importance of church hierarchy.

This series of events led to a reduction in the numbers of BECs. They were no longer formally supported by many of the parishes and dioceses. Many of them continued to meet but outside any church structure.[44] Although researchers who study BECs today tend to emphasize their shrinking numbers, they still exist. 'Studies place the number of base communities throughout Brazil somewhere between 80–100,000 . . . between 3 and 8% of the national Catholic population' (Vásquez,[45] 1998, p. 57). With these numbers remaining, there should still be a significant amount of liberation theology being created. Yet, part of the problem of the formalization of liberation theology is that liberation theologians moved away from the direct creation of theology by the communities themselves.[46]

This was an extremely difficult time for Latin American liberation theologians. Not only were they being repressed by governments and rejected by the Vatican but the political system was shifting around them and they were caught short with their focus on the economic realm. In the 1980s, there was a move toward democracy. Yet, the economic discussion did not open up. It still focused on achieving capitalist development through economic growth.

Latin American liberation theologians who began to work with the language of the North, attempting to counter both capitalism and communism, found themselves adrift in their search for a third way. With the shift in the global political situation around 1990, the language in the North changed to that of globalization.[47] Yet, this concept of global

---

44 Although not part of the ecclesial structure, they still merge faith and reality, as CEAS shows.

45 Manuel Vásquez is professor of religion in Latin America.

46 Some argue this model may not be possible in the current phase of globalization. 'In the face of this chaotic situation, it has become less and less plausible to claim, as do liberation theology and the popular church, that Brazilians can become the "artisans of their own destiny", that they can, by their own efforts, make their society more rational, just, and egalitarian' (Vásquez, 1998, p. 4).

47 They argued capitalism could be assumed because communism had failed; socialism was ignored.

capitalism had been rejected more than 30 years before by many liberationists.

How were the liberation theologians to respond? In the face of the global economic system, it appeared that liberation theology may have become irrelevant. 'Liberation theology has failed to respond to the new reality in Latin America, preserving many utopian themes which now lack credibility' (Forrester and Kee in Vásquez, 1998, p. x). People were powerless under the military government, where they could not participate as citizens. Theoretically, this avenue had been opened with the return of democratic government.

Latin American liberation theology continued to call for alternatives to the current system. When merged with development critics and the experiences of others around the world its relevance reappears.

## Themes taken forward[48]

Latin American liberation theologians continued to assume a bias toward the poor. They defined sin as injustice and salvation as liberation from sin. They defined justice in light of salvation, the struggle toward a new heaven and a new earth. In terms of human action toward justice, economically the wealth of the rich needed to be reduced. As it expanded to other realms, the argument became: the powerful should give up their power. And finally, their goal was to build human community. With each of these themes, there was movement beyond the confines of Latin America and beyond the economic realm, as Christians around the world reflected on similar themes.

### A bias toward the poor

For liberation theologians, the poor remained the starting point for theology. The 'theological and social location for the Christian are one,

---

48 For details of these themes see the series of volumes on Theology and Liberation published by Burns & Oates, UK and Orbis Books, USA. See also the base community described in Urban Rural Mission, 1988.

unified in the specific commitment to the poor' (Bonino,[49] 1983, p. 44). In order to know God, Christians must be in relationship with the poor.

Beginning theology with the poor challenged those who held power in any realm. The powerless called the powerful to repentance, to end their sinfulness.

> Commitment to the poor and oppressed and the rise of grassroots communities have helped the church to discover the evangelizing potential of the poor. For the poor challenge the church constantly, summoning it to conversion; and many of the poor incarnate in their lives the evangelical values of solidarity, service, simplicity, and openness to accepting the gift of God. (Gutiérrez in Nickoloff, 1986, p. 113)[50]

The poor were instruments of conversion. Liberation theology continued to argue that injustice between the rich and the poor signified unjust relationships with God. Injustice had to be eradicated to build right relationships between human beings and with God.[51]

### Sin as injustice: idolatry

Sin was injustice and injustice was powerlessness. '"Poor" in the biblical sense, denotes the dominated, oppressed, humiliated, instrumentalized term of the practical relationship called sin' (Dussel, 1988, p. 22). The poor lacked justice.

---

49 José Miguez Bonino is an Argentine Methodist liberation theologian.

50 Gutiérrez is quoting article 1147 from the Puebla document 'A Preferential Option for the Poor'.

51 Two examples are of race and sex. Althaus-Reid has developed Indecent Theology, exploring the intersection between liberation and queer theology. 'An Indecent Theology will question the traditional Latin American field of decency and order as it permeates and supports the multiple . . . structures of life in my country, Argentina, and my continent' (Althaus-Reid, 2000c, p. 2). See her *Indecent Theology* for further explication. Second, regarding race, a South African black theology of liberation emerged, dealing with the intersection of liberation and race. See, for example, Simon Maimela's 'A Black Theology of Liberation'.

In the economic realm, having riches resulted from a situation of injustice. Dussel explained, 'when a shoemaker exchanges shoes for bread, a relationship between persons arises' (Dussel, 1988, p. 79). How did this relationship become sinful? 'The origin of evil or sin lies in a negation of the other, the other person' (p. 18). Instead of doing what would be best for the other person, the focus changed to oneself. I, as an individual, regarded myself as more important than the other. The other person became an object at my service. This domination was evidence of idolatry. The aim of human community should be to worship God in relationship with each other. Forgetting this, individuals placed themselves first.

Where human beings were formerly treated as persons, they became 'things'. Oppositely, money changed from an idea into a person, central to society (Althaus-Reid, 2000a, p. 48). Liberation theologians began to argue that as labour became money, money became prioritized over people. 'Everything produced seems purchasable . . . [even] the producers themselves' (Hinkelammert, 1986, p. 24). All that is left for humanity is the choice of what and who to consume.

The workers did not even keep the money their labour has turned into, the owners did.[52] Any profit was taken from another person's life. 'The act by which one asserts oneself as the end of other persons – as factory owners think they have a right to the factory's profit even though that profit be their workers' hunger transformed into money – is idolatry' (Dussel, 1988, p. 19). Those who were rich economically were only rich through this domination. The current economic system excluded people in favour of money and found this to be acceptable.

The choice was between life and death: God was the way of life and Mammon was the way of death.[53]

---

52 For example, the workers could be the owners of a business. One example of such a business is John Lewis in the UK. For more information on John Lewis see http://www.john-lewis-partnership.co.uk.

53 Secular practitioners also distinguished between the choice of life or death. Following out the 'deadly tale inspired by the basic precepts of Newtonian physics . . . led to the embrace of money as the defining value of contemporary societies and given birth to a hedonistic ethic of material self-gratification; the hierarchical,

Money only works while people trust it to, and nobody can trust it to work if they do not believe others will continue to trust it to do so . . . At some point . . . the faith we place in money becomes something more than the trust we put in the instruments of our everyday life . . . or the trust we rightly place in our fellow human beings, and becomes more like the trust which I believe belongs to God alone. (Selby, 1998, p. 76)[54]

When humans put their trust in money before God, that was idolatry. Mammon did not have to rule the exchange of money.[55] Similar arguments have been made for other realms. Mammon is not the only god we worship.

What then was the way of life for liberation theologians? It was justice in community, as the final section argues. Society should be based in community.[56]

---

control-oriented megainstitutions of the state and the corporation; and an economic system that rewards greed and destroys life' (Korten, 1999, pp. 9–10). This story of competition turned out to be the wrong one. The new story said 'the universe is a self-organizing system engaged in the discovery and realization of its possibilities through a continuing process of transcendence toward ever higher levels of order and self-definition' (p. 12). Instead of emphasizing death, it emphasized life: co-operation in community.

54  Peter Selby is an Anglican bishop.

55  The example of usury (interest) shows how the choice of life, the worship of God above money, could impact policy. In early Christian traditions, usury was a sin. Islam has retained its prohibition on usury. Some Christian theologians continue to argue that usury is sinful. If the practice of interest were to end, it would have enormous implications for the global economy.

56  Alasdair McIntosh, a Scottish community activist and liberation theologian, presented the following options. With mutuality, a fisherman gave fish and the recipient gave some eggs in return but only if able to do so. In reciprocity, the fisherman gave fish when it was reciprocated with eggs. However, the eggs would still come when the fishing was bad. In bartering, the formula became set with perhaps one fish for three eggs. But then came rigidity, 'if I have fish to trade but you don't want eggs, we cannot do business' (McIntosh, 2001, p. 30). Thus, entered money.

## Liberation as justice in community

### A new heaven and a new earth

Analysing the new heaven and the new earth, God's kingdom, helped liberation theologians to explore the concept of justice. 'The kingdom or reign of God means the full and total liberation of all creation, in the end, purified of all that oppresses it, transfigured by the full presence of God' (Boff and Boff, 1987, p. 52). The kingdom was liberation.

First, they argued the kingdom was both spiritual and material. 'The kingdom of God is something more than historical liberations, which are always limited and open to further perfectioning, but it is anticipated and incarnated in them in time, in preparation for its full realization with the coming of the new heaven and the new earth' (Boff and Boff, 1987, p. 53). God's work and God's new earth were not solely spiritual concepts that existed outside of history but they were spiritual and material concepts that existed within history.

Second, it was God's reign but it also required human action. 'The kingdom is a gift, a *grace* of God, but also a *demand* made upon us' (Gutiérrez in Nickoloff, 1996, p. 173). Working toward the new earth was a crucial part of an active Christian life, not an option.[57]

Third, God's reign would be introduced fully in the future but it was also present now. 'It is not a kingdom "of this world" (John 18.36), but it nevertheless begins to come about in this world' (Boff and Boff, 1987, p. 52). The new earth was not only something looked toward but also through Christian action the new earth was already appearing.[58] The

---

57 This action stemmed directly from the example of Jesus. Although Jesus proclaimed that God would bring about the kingdom, he still acted while on this earth to bring about change.

58 Segundo argued, 'Every such happening (a liberative event) . . . stands in a causal relationship to the definitive kingdom. The causality is partial, fragile, often distorted and in need of reworking; but it is a far cry from being nothing more than an anticipation, outline, or analogy of the kingdom. We definitely are not talking about the latter when we are talking about such option as racial segregation versus community of rights, laissez-faire supply and demand in international trade versus a truly balanced marketing process . . . In however fragmentary a way, what is

alternatives would only fully replace the existing system when God's new earth arrived, as Christ's time on earth confirmed. Jesus encouraged the introduction of a new earth in opposition to the current society. His crucifixion and death was due to the challenge he made to those in power.[59] Jesus overcame those who killed him by coming back to life, showing the limits to the power of the current system. The earthly authorities would not succeed because God would one day introduce the new earth.

Finally, the central value of the struggle for the new earth was justice. 'Liberation, the practice of justice, the construction of the Reign is not optional' (Sobrino, 1996, p. 72). Christians, in working toward the new earth, had to aim for justice.

How should Christians act to bring about justice? First, the powerful needed to give up their power. Let's take three brief examples:[60] the Sabbath and Jubilee legislation, God's ownership of the earth, and principalities and powers. Each of these suggested practice for the economic realm but can also be expanded to other realms.

### Sabbath and Jubilee legislation

In the narrative of biblical radicalism, economic justice is the fundamental social goal of the people of God. The ancient vision of the Jubilee year . . . was periodically to deconstruct debt, land alienation,

---

involved is the eschatological kingdom itself, whose revelation and realization is anxiously awaited by the whole universe' (Segundo, 1980, pp. 257–8).

59 See the later section on principalities and powers. Crucifixion was the punishment for those who flouted Rome's authority. 'Although some would still view Jesus as an innocuous religious teacher, it is becoming increasingly evident to many that he catalyzed a movement of the renewal of Israel – a movement over against Roman rule as well as the Jerusalem priestly aristocracy' (Horsley, 1997, p. 1). Richard Horsley is a biblical scholar and religion professor.

60 There are many more examples but these three have been linked to particular practices. The Sabbath and Jubilee legislation has been linked to relieving the debt crisis; God's ownership of the earth has been linked to ecology and land reform; principalities and powers have been linked to changing international structures like the World Bank and the WTO.

and bond servitude – the three stages of impoverishment resulting from indebtedness . . . We who have been socialized within the womb of capitalism dismiss such notions as utopian . . . But this attitude is precisely what is at issue in the conclusion to [the story of the rich man]. (Gorringe, 1997, p. 41)[61]

The Sabbath and Jubilee years in the Old Testament focused on reintroducing justice in community.[62] In the Sabbath year, every seventh year, people and the land were to rest. The poor were allowed to harvest the fields of the rich, as a way of redistributing wealth. In addition, debts were to be released.

The Jubilee year introduced a more extensive redistribution of wealth as a way to re-establish justice. Land was initially distributed equally in community. However, over time some would grow richer and others poorer, losing their land and often having to labour for others. Every fiftieth year, ownership of one's labour, land, and home returned to its original distribution. The goal was justice for every human being, which was seen to require equal distribution of resources.[63]

In the New Testament, the life and words of Jesus reinforced the Jubilee aim for justice.[64] Redistribution was to be practised on a daily basis, not every 7 or 49 years. 'Jesus is putting the structural justice of socio-economic reality at the heart of his mission, at the heart of the inauguration of the reign of God, the agenda of kingdom ethics' (Grey, 2000, p. 80). For Grey, because Luke addressed his text to the rich, the message of redistribution was not just to give hope to the poor but was intended to change the lives of the rich as well.

The Jubilee legislation was based on God's ownership of the earth.

---

61 Gorringe is quoting Ched Myers, 1994, *Who Will Roll Away the Stone?* New York: Orbis, pp. 166-7.

62 See, for example, Leviticus 25 and Deuteronomy 15.1-11.

63 This call for Jubilee has been used to support debt relief. See *Proclaim Liberty* (Christian Aid, 1998) and Northcott, *Life After Debt*. See Selby, *Grace and Mortgage* for a wider analysis of debt. Michael Northcott is an Anglican theologian and reader in Christian ethics.

64 See Luke 4.18-30.

## God's ownership of the earth

God owns the earth and all its resources; humans do not.[65] Part of human sinfulness was to claim ownership over what is God's. God's ownership of the earth called for limits on human ownership.[66] The notion of property implied a particular relationship between human beings, as the analysis of justice showed. Property separated people from full community. 'I am only rich or poor, a possessor or indigent, in relation to others' (Gorringe, 1994, p. 127). If there were no other people around, then property would not be an issue. However, at its base, considering one person to have ownership of a piece of land denied justice. Property was not owned by the rich for them to be charitable with. Instead, it should belong to all in common and be shared justly.

Their definition of justice became clearer. These theologians argued that charity should be subsumed in the struggle for justice. First, charity simply should not exist. The rich did not own the property they claimed to own. Miranda[67] explained that the Hebrew word translated as charity was in fact the same word as for justice. 'Almsgiving for the original Bible was a restitution that someone makes for something that is not his' (Miranda, 1977, p. 15). The poor should have the same access to the earth's resources as the rich. What did the verse 'you shall not steal' mean?[68] Property obtained from the labour of others is stealing. If I claimed the right of ownership to a piece of property,

I am being blind to the fact that private property denied to the workers whose labor has produced it is unjustified accumulation, taking over

---

65 Psalm 24.1 states that 'the earth is the Lord's and all that is in it, the world, and those who live in it.'

66 From an ecological perspective, the lack of limits, alongside the assumption of human ownership of the earth, caused destruction. Treating it as God's, to be shared among all humans, could change the situation. Ecotheology has dealt with this further. Publications include John Cobb, Jr's (1995) *Is It Too Late?*, Leonardo Boff's *Ecology and Liberation*, and Hallman's *Ecotheology: Voices from South and North*.

67 José Miranda is a Mexican biblical scholar and liberation theologian.

68 We saw the beginnings of this interpretation in *Gaudium et Spes*.

the capital of the fruits of their labor, previously stolen from them without my being conscious of the theft. (Dussel, 1988, p. 33)

It was the rich who stole from the poor by claiming ownership.

This led to the second point. There would be no need for charity because there would be justice. When the situation began to be unjust, the property would be redistributed. 'It is easier for a camel to go through the eye of a needle than for a rich man to go into the kingdom of heaven' (Matthew 19.24). A rich man could not enter heaven. Having riches was sinful. It was not about the rich man abusing his power of ownership but 'against differentiating ownership itself' (Miranda, 1977, p. 18). It followed then that giving food to those who are hungry and drink to those who are thirsty was not optional but required in order to restore justice.

These theologians argued that there can be no justice in the capitalist system. They were particularly critical of the focus on the individual in capitalism, which led to the destruction of community. In order to define justice, the entire society or community had to be considered.

*Principalities and powers*

These themes have so far focused on the economic realm. However, all structures of sin (economic, political, social, racial, and so forth) were critiqued. All structures should aim toward justice; all should worship God. Structures needed to be redeemed, converted to their true purpose. Salvation should mean an end to all sin, both individual and structural. Yet many Christians continued to participate in sinful structures.[69]

Consideration of the wider context of principalities and powers contributed further to the analysis of structures. First, as with the new heaven and the new earth, the principalities and powers were both spiritual and material. Walter Wink[70] argued that 'every Power tends to have

---

69 People then sinned as individuals through their participation in these structures.

70 Wink, professor of biblical interpretation, published *Naming the Powers* (1984), *Unmasking the Powers* (1986) and *Engaging the Powers* (1992).

a visible pole, an outer form – be it a church, a nation, or an economy – and an invisible pole, an inner spirit or driving force that animates, legitimates, and regulates its physical manifestation in the world (Wink, 1984, p. 5). Both existed together and should be treated together.

Second, liberation theologians argued that Christian communities should struggle with these structures because the structures no longer worship God. 'While questioning a system's economic and political structures, we must always ask what in fact "functions" as God' (Duchrow, 1995, p. 205). In the capitalist system, for example, God was replaced by money. The structures' idolatry of Mammon did not mean that they were irretrievably evil. However, they were sinning, having forgotten their God-given purpose.

They are good in that we need mechanisms by which people can be clothed, housed and fed, and by which human ingenuity can be channelled for the common good. They are fallen in that they are used for the profit of the few. (Gorringe, 2000a, p. 94)

They should be mechanisms for equality, if they rejected the focus on profit, choosing to serve God not Mammon.

So how could the powers be redeemed? 'The church's task is to unmask this idolatry and recall the Powers to their created purposes in the world' (Wink, 1984, p. 5). The principalities and powers could be transformed. They could follow the example set by Jesus. 'The words and deeds of Jesus reveal that he is not a minor reformer but an egalitarian prophet who repudiated the very premises of the Domination System: the right of some to lord it over others by means of power, wealth, shaming, or titles' (Wink, 1998, p. 65). Jesus wanted power to be shared in community and set the possibility in motion.[71]

---

71 Jesus' crucifixion and death showed how the principalities and powers react to the possibility of being transformed. 'Pilate reminds him (Jesus): "Do you not know that I have power to release you, and power to crucify you?" (John 19.10). Jesus replied that this power of Pilate's was "from above", that it came from God, that Pilate was responsible to God' (Forrester, 1988, p. 18). Although Pilate did not find Jesus guilty of any crime, Jesus was still executed. The principalities and

Solidarity and resistance by local communities could help to redeem the principalities and powers. 'Confronting such a regime and recalling it to its true role is a special responsibility for Christians because they alone have a knowledge of the christological foundation and the divine mandate of the state' (Forrester, 1989, p. 72). This required action in the socio-political and spiritual realms and fundamental changes to the structures. This is the work liberation theologians can continue in every realm, basing their work in communities of the excluded.

Christian communities could provide a model toward which the structures can aim. Christianity was about co-operating to help bring about the new earth. A sharing of power in just community was considered the basis of God's new earth.

*Liberation: community*

So how could Christians go about rebuilding their communities in practice? The building of community had to begin in reality: physical, environmental, and social reality.[72] 'God's dream of justice for the whole of creation' includes 'a re-ordering of relations which includes humanity's relations with nature and the environment' (Grey, 1997, p. 108).

---

powers saw a challenge to their authority and tried to end it. Yet, God overcame the powers. This interpretation of Jesus' death and resurrection is not the one most frequently used today. So why did it change over time? Christianity became intertwined with the ruling system in the fourth century. 'Called on to legitimate the empire, the church abandoned much of its social critique. The Powers were soon divorced from political affairs . . . the state was thus freed of one of the most powerful brakes against idolatry' (Wink, 1984, p. 113). Christians then changed the emphasis of the crucifixion and resurrection of Christ. The church 'took the Powers off the hook' and 'argued that God is the one who provided Jesus as a Lamb, . . . that God is the angry and aggrieved party who must be placated' (Wink, 1998, p. 87). This understanding remains prominent today. Instead, Christians should struggle against the unjust principalities and powers. Duncan Forrester is a Scottish political theologian.

72 Grey argues that the first step in building community is to dwell there (Grey, 1997). I use her model of dwelling, tradition, transformation, and imagination as a framework for this discussion.

Dwelling in community included respecting the environment, God's creation.[73]

Liberation communities focused on the building of a relationship between humans and God through their relations with each other. Where there was the praxis of domination in the sinful systems, the alternative through conscientization would be the praxis of love. This love is 'love for the other     for the sake of that other', including 'delight, beauty, goodness and holiness' (Dussel, 1988, p. 10). In just communities, each person was concerned for the other, not for the individual alone.

Just community was crucial because it is only through just community that people could know and love God. 'We meet God in our encounter with others' (Gutiérrez in Nickoloff, 1996, p. 150). It was not possible to know God otherwise. In particular, they were to prioritize the excluded, 'those whose human features have been disfigured by oppression, despoilation, and alienation and who have "no beauty, no majesty" but are the things "from which men turn away their eyes" (Isa. 53.2-3)' (p. 155). Every person had to be treated justly in community in order for God to be present.

In rebuilding community, people did not start with a clean slate. Tradition was a crucial resource. 'Never has there been a greater need for the recovery of solidarity with the past struggles to create authentic ecclesia, communities of justice, of truth and fidelity to the vision of the Kingdom of God' (Grey, 1997, p. 82). The Christian Church had a long history of working toward God's new earth beginning with Christ.

Jesus' life and actions and the earliest Christian communities[74] could be a model for Christians today. They were 'the salt, light and leaven of the kingdom of God in Israel and among the peoples' (Duchrow, 1995,

---

73 Again, issues of ecology and sustainability arise here.

74 Paul's creation of Christian communities after Jesus' death and resurrection provided a model for working toward God's reign on earth. 'The principal term Paul uses with reference both to the movement as a whole and to the particular local communities is *ekklesia*', which is normally translated as church (Horsley, 1997, p. 208). However, the new communities were an alternative to the entire economic, political, and cultural system.

p. 180). These communities showed how justice would rule in God's new earth.

The sharing of the Eucharist, for example, provided a model for how sharing could occur in community. 'Communion is the capacity for establishing interpersonal relationships, for nourishing spirituality . . . (to) build up human community' (Boff, 1995, p. 107). First, the Eucharist was not complete with one individual. It was communion, a means of forming community. Second, bread was at the centre, suggesting economic and political components.

> In sharing bread, we remember the love and trust of Jesus who was taken to His death, and the confirmation of His mission towards the poor through the resurrection. The breaking of bread is both the point of departure and the destination of the Christian community. This act represents the profound communion with human suffering caused in many cases by the lack of bread, and it is the recognition, in joy, of the Resurrected Jesus who gives life and lifts the hopes of the people brought together by his acts and his word. (Gutiérrez, 1999, p. 37)

In order to celebrate the Eucharist, there had to be bread to be shared. Someone had to bake this bread, a material action. Third, when the bread was produced it had to be distributed. 'The question arises how to share it . . . the temptation arises not to share it (sin), and the need arises to celebrate it, for the gladness that the bread produces' (Sobrino, 1996, p. 67). It was given, exchanged, or sold to the community that was participating in the Eucharist. Fourth, in order for the bread of the Eucharist to be just, it had to be produced justly; it could not be the product of exploitation. Using the product of exploitation to celebrate the Eucharist was to bring the celebration of injustice into the Eucharist itself.[75]

Fifth, for a just Eucharist, not only were the goods made and shared

---

75 Regarding consumption, Christians should take as much care over all consumption as they do over the Eucharist because the material and the spiritual are intertwined.

fairly, but each person participated.[76] No one was to be excluded from God's communities.[77] Sixth, this consumption of the Eucharist was not limited to those with money. 'All are invited freely to this meal' (Meeks, 1989, p. 179). Everyone shared in the consumption equally. Seventh, this just sharing prioritized the poor. Participating in the Eucharist included being aware 'of all those others who are also invited to share the meaning of all social goods through Christ's body, namely, the poor, the oppressed, the sinners, and the dying' (p. 179). If no one was to be excluded from the Eucharist, then no one should be excluded from other forms of community.

Yet tradition was not enough on its own to rebuild community; transformation was also crucial. 'Transforming society in the name of the ethics of the Kingdom, through its witness to truth and justice, is the most cherished part of the Church's mission' (Grey, 1997, p. 92). The Christian tradition of struggling toward God's new earth had to continue to transform communities. They could not be satisfied with the *status quo* because the new earth was not yet fully present.

Finally, these just communities required imagination (Grey, 1997). Because the new earth was not yet fully present, it had to be envisioned. This imagination was part of the process of action and reflection. Liberation theologians argued that the base communities could be models for working toward God's new earth in community.[78]

Linking back to our discussion of alternatives, the prioritization of community over the individual would lead to changes in every realm. For

---

76 It is, of course, limited to Christians. Another challenge for liberation theology, as CEAS argues, is to stop prioritizing Christians.

77 This just community should extend beyond the boundaries of the Eucharist to Christians in their daily lives. As the Eucharist does not rely on money, could the economy, or society in general, possibly rely on something other than money? 'Human need, when connected with money as the depository of value as such, justifies dominative and exploitative relationships as natural' (Meeks, 1989, p. 168). In contrast, God's body and blood are shared freely with all; no one is entitled to more than another.

78 This alternative included conscientization and expanded to all practice of the process of action and reflection.

example, 'the goal of the economy could be the building up of communities rather than the expansion of markets' (Cobb, 1994, pp. 10-11). When
community is prioritized, the orientation of the economy moves away
from the individual, profit and growth. The starting point shifts from the
individual who competes with others to the community that shares its
resources. There are alternative economic models already available that
are based in community. In this case, then, there appears to be a direct
correlation between the theological and the policy concepts of theologians and practitioners.

The analysis of community also impacts the political realm. For example, democracy could be redefined. 'Democracy, as envisaged now by so
many groups in Latin America, is based on the co-existence and articula-
tion of five founding forces: participation, solidarity, equality, difference,
and communion' (Boff, 1995, p. 105). People have to be able to particu-
late in community. People have to co-operate. People have to show love
for each other. And there must be diversity. A just community then could
be democratic, allowing each person to participate. In a democratic
system, citizens have the opportunity to participate equally. However,
the decentralization of power has to be ensured even within democracies
and not assumed.

And these two realms cannot be addressed alone. People are impover-
ished due to race, gender, and sexual orientation, as well as in other ways.
In a just community, inequality will not exist. 'None of us can realise
Jesus' promise of "life in all its fullness" while some of us suffer violence,
hunger, homelessness, torture, poverty-linked illness, marginalisation or
environmental degradation' (White and Tiongco, 1997, p. 15).[79] Living
in just community requires prioritizing the poor. And so we come full
circle to the beginning.

---

79 Sarah White is Director of a Centre for Development Studies. Romy
Tiongco is a Filipino Catholic liberation theologian, former Christian Aid partner,
and former Christian Aid staff member. Where I situate these themes in a theology
of liberation, White and Tiongco discussed them as theology and development
together. Yet, their themes of power, participation, gender and violence all drew
on themes in liberation theologies.

## Context in the North: Christian Aid

Despite the emergence of liberation theologies in many contexts around the world and the formalization of liberation theology in Latin America, the North seemed determined to press forward with its acceptance of a global capitalist system. These theologies were ignored in the dominant discourse, or their language was co-opted. Development seemed to be left out of the theological discussion. Yet, agencies like Christian Aid work toward development within 'globalization'. The question for our purposes is, since the criticism of development fit with themes in liberation and since there was no theology of development that emerged, does this mean development has to be rejected by Christians? Let's explore what concepts from the previous two chapters emerge from the context of Christian Aid. How do they work from their faith base? What is the situation of faith, development and liberation now?

## Conclusion

Liberation theology was not dead, as some had argued. Latin American liberation theology itself has been formalized and it has inspired other communities around the world to reflect on their own situations. Liberation theologies dealing with racism, sexism, heterosexism and other 'isms' have emerged. In this context, the voices in the North calling for alternatives and the voices in the South calling for alternatives perhaps could speak together. Both secular calls for alternatives and liberationists argue that alternatives should be holistic and not simply prioritize the economic realm. While rejected by dominant discourse, they have continued to flourish.

Liberation theologies continue to call for a bias toward those marginalized or excluded in whatever context. Sin is injustice; salvation and liberation are the practice of justice. And within this praxis is the building of community.

So with this knowledge of the status of globalization and liberation, let's turn to the case of Christian Aid.

# Part III

## *Here and Now*

# 5

# A Case Study – Christian Aid:
# Faith, Development, Globalization
# and Trade

## Introduction

How do faith-based aid agencies justify their development practice today
when there is no overtly supportive theology? This chapter presents an
analysis of one faith-based agency, Christian Aid.[1] Christian Aid works
within the field of development: engaging in development practice and in
advocacy. A recent advocacy focus was the international trade campaign.
For Christian Aid, the development paradigm and the phenomenon of
globalization, if managed properly, can be positive.

Christian Aid analyses its practice theologically. It claims to use the
hermeneutical circle from liberation theology.[2] Yet, many Christian Aid

---

1 Christian Aid and CEAS cannot be taken as representative of all agencies.
Others would need to take this research further in these and other agencies again
in the future as the situation changes. One reason Christian Aid can be illustrative
is that its directors over the years have remained vocal about merging theology and
development. Charles Elliott, as we saw, was involved with the WCC and then
directed Christian Aid. Michael Taylor then directed Christian Aid from 1985 to
1997. We have also seen work from Tiongco, a former Christian Aid staff member
and partner. It is this locus that could help to move forward from the stalled position. From the chapters so far, it appears that a decision has to be made: does the
Christian mandate urge us to reject development for justice or does it urge us to
ignore development and focus on capitalism?

2 In Christian Aid's case its communities are regional workshops, working
groups, conferences and other meetings.

staff and supporters expect the theology to support development practice, as we saw in the beginnings of the call for a theology of development. Having seen their practice and method, we can then turn to the theological issues emerging. For Christian Aid, the theological reflection is set in the context of a struggle toward a new earth. Justice is the central goal of this struggle. To move toward justice, Christian Aid reflects theologically on the concepts of community. There is an issue-based theology emerging from reflection in community. At the same time, there is a divide between the method of liberation theology and their attempts to merge it with development practice.

Thus, this chapter addresses the following questions. How does Christian Aid define and practise development and globalization?[3] How does Christian Aid merge faith with practice? And finally, what theology supports its actions?

## Development, globalization and trade

Globalisation is a process of increasing interconnectedness of individuals, groups, companies and countries . . . Some form of globalisation is a given. But globalisation is not the same as the weather – it can be managed. As the Secretary of State for International Development has repeatedly pointed out, globalisation has been designed by people, and can be reformed by people. The important question is how can it be made to work most effectively for poor people? (Green and Melamed, 2000, p. 1)[4]

Christian Aid situates its discussion of development in the larger context

---

3 This chapter examines only Christian Aid's advocacy. They do not 'practise' development themselves; their role in the development process is to fund agencies in the south, who define development in different ways. They advocate in the North on behalf of these partners and the UK churches. Some of their partners reject the term 'development' in its entirety, as we will see with the case of CEAS.

4 Duncan Green was a CAFOD staff member and Claire Melamed was Senior Policy Officer for Trade and Globalization at Christian Aid.

of globalization.[5] They begin with a definition of 'increasing interconnectedness'.[6] The upsurge in economic interconnectedness has two characteristics, according to Christian Aid. There has been an increase in the speed and scale of economic activity.[7]

For Christian Aid, this process of globalization is irreversible. Thus, it has to be dealt with; it cannot be ignored or rejected. Christian Aid policy advocates a situation of managed globalization. They argue that the globalization of the capitalist economy does not need to be rejected but it does need to be reformed;[8] the benefits of globalization need to be distributed among the poor. We can see this view clearly in their recent advocacy on international trade.

*Trade for Life*

I believe trade should work in the interests of all people. I promise to act with others to change the rules that govern international trade so that they work to eradicate poverty, protect the environment and

---

5 While the practice of Christian Aid is to let its partners define development, one staff member commenting on one of my PhD chapters, stated: 'What I mean by development is a dual process of growth and poverty reduction.'

6 Christian Aid emphasizes the 'technological, economic, and political' interconnectedness that results from the globalization of various phenomena (Green and Melamed, 1). Yet their focus too remains on the economic realm. The political realm is discussed where that realm interacts with the economy. This definition of globalization is different from the dictionary definition of a 'making worldwide in scope or application'. So, is it an increasing interconnectedness of economies, for example? Or is it a 'making worldwide' of one particular type of economy, as we saw critics argue?

7 Money now moves around the world with the touch of a computer key. Due to the increased speed and scale of economic activity there is less individual country control over events. For example, the downturn in the Japanese economy in 1998 affected the Scottish whisky industry because Japan previously imported a lot of Scottish whisky.

8 DfID made a similar argument, although their suggestions for the management of the global economy differed. They assumed that effective governments and efficient markets would benefit the poor.

ensure equal access to life in all its fullness. (Christian Aid Trade Campaign Pledge)

International trade became an advocacy focus because of its centrality to the process of globalization. 'Trading relationships are now shaped by the technological, political, and economic changes that together are called "globalisation".' (Melamed and MacMullan,[9] 2000, p. 3). Christian Aid began to campaign on trade in order to marshal support from supporters and partners to change current international trade policies.

The name 'Trade for Life' emphasizes two characteristics of the campaign. First is that trade can be positive. 'We believe that the right kind of trade can and must be part of the solution to poverty' (Trade for Life [2000], p. 1). From Christian Aid's perspective, trade is a starting point for the process of development. As Mukarji stated in his interview, excerpted in the introduction, developing countries want to be part of the international trading system.[10]

However, trade is currently unjust. 'Some people are not able to trade as much as they would like, while others are forced into trading relationships that they don't benefit from' (Melamed and MacMullan, 2000, 3).[11] Trade is not leading to improved livelihoods because people are not free to choose when, how, and how much to trade. The campaign aims 'to ensure that trade works in the interests of everyone, not just the few' (p. 3). In the situation of just trade, which Christian Aid advocates, the poor benefit from trade.

The second characteristic emerging from the campaign name is its emphasis on life. It reiterates Christian Aid's traditional focus on life before death, reflecting not only policy but theological undertones as

---

9 Justin MacMullan was a Campaigns Officer.

10 The policy and campaigns teams use evidence from partners around the world to explain this focus. Partners like CEAS, however, reject a focus on trade. In fact, when CEAS received the Christian Aid material on the trade campaign (in English), it was mentioned briefly at team leaders' meeting and then filed.

11 The negative effects of trade have been addressed by several aid agencies. For example, see Madeley, 1999. John Madeley was a Christian Aid staff member.

well. This characteristic forms the basis for the theological reflection in the following section.

There are two main objectives for the trade campaign: changing the rules of international trade, decided in the WTO, and regulating the TNCs, the most powerful actors in international trade.[12] Although international trade is often publicized as a situation of free trade, there are rules guiding the process. These rules are created by the interaction of governments in the WTO.[13] Christian Aid's trade campaign is critical of the current international trade rules, calling them deadly. These deadly rules should be changed to become rules that enhance life. For example, the first deadly rule ensures that poor countries cannot protect their domestic markets from cheap food imported from other countries. Countries in the North can export their excess food production to poorer Southern countries. Because of this inexpensive imported food, poor countries are unable to build up their own food production.

In changing this rule to emphasize life rather than death, poor countries would be able to protect themselves from imports of food they have the ability to produce on their own. A poor country could ensure that its

---

12 Christian Aid supporters can use their economic power to meet these two objectives. For example, during the Fair Trade campaign, Christian Aid campaigners collected their supermarket till receipts and presented them to store managers in groups, emphasizing that they would spend their money in any supermarket that stocked fairly traded goods and signed up to the Ethical Trading Initiative. See Christian Aid, 1999b. However, in this campaign it is political power that is crucial. They want to ensure that the UK government represents their views at the WTO, the World Bank, and the IMF. Thus, MPs, MSPs, and MEPs are active targets for the campaigners. An MP is a Member of the UK Parliament; an MSP is a Member of the Scottish Parliament, and an MEP is a Member of the European Parliament. Christian Aid's website has examples of several positive outcomes that have been achieved so far. While on their own they may not be able to change the situation, they aim to build an alliance through the Trade Justice Movement that will work to change the UK government first. This aspect of exercising citizenship is absent from the theological reflection but is central to CEAS as the next chapter shows.

13 The rules in place today prioritize the rich but should prioritize the poor. This call for a bias toward the poor merges with the theological reflection.

own farmers are able to develop their production. It would retain control over its own food production rather than being reliant on imports from other countries.[14]

While the WTO is the place where these rules are agreed, the IMF, the World Bank and the UK government are all campaign targets because of their ability to influence the rule-making.[15] Instead of being forced to follow the deadly rules, Christian Aid argues that countries should be encouraged by the World Bank and the IMF to draw up their own development strategies.

Christian Aid also emphasizes that it is crucial for the UK government to change its own policies on international trade before taking the lead in influencing the WTO to change. 'The UK's trade with developing countries is worth around 300 billion pounds per year – over 100 times the value of UK government aid' (Green and Melamed, 2000, p. 38). For Christian Aid, if UK trade policy aimed for poverty eradication that would be far more effective than UK aid for development.

Christian Aid is particularly concerned that countries retain sovereignty over their citizens, markets and resources.[16] Limiting the power of TNCs is crucial to retaining a nation's sovereignty. TNCs are also structures that can either contribute to poverty or work to eradicate it, according to Christian Aid. Christian Aid emphasizes that the TNCs in and of themselves are not inevitably harmful to the poor. They can and should prioritize the poor.[17] Christian Aid's second campaign objective is to regulate these TNCs.

---

14 For further details on each of these rules and the changes suggested by Christian Aid, see Curtis, *Trade for Life*. Mark Curtis was head of global advocacy and policy at Christian Aid.

15 Remember that the World Bank and the IMF currently impose conditions on their loans and grants to developing countries, which require these countries to follow WTO rules.

16 Its focus on country sovereignty makes one crucial assumption: that each country will have a successfully functioning democratic government. CEAS, in contrast, does not make this assumption. Where Christian Aid emphasizes trade rather than citizenship, citizenship is central to CEAS.

17 In contrast, others argue that it is impossible for TNCs to benefit the poor, and so they should be dismantled.

the Holy Spirit, that strengthens us and gives us this force; and also to struggle, that gives such strength to the desire that, at the same time that you don't want to, you go! So, first I have to ask God, I pray before I leave the house, ask the Divine Holy Spirit to accompany me and I go. Sometimes, I nearly break my heart, but I go there into the struggle, to raise the state of mind of the other washwomen. (Debate [2001], p. 72)

While the 'struggle' can be expressed in theological or Christian terms, there is not necessarily a distinction made between the theological and the non-theological. Faith blends in with praxis, determines praxis, and is determined by praxis.

It is in this context that base communities can be redefined. They do still exist, although they are not exclusively ecclesial. A flexible definition is needed to encompass groups that acknowledge a linking spirituality throughout different faiths and those that may reflect on values not linked to a particular faith.

There is a complex relationship in Brazil, and in this case in Bahia, between the African-Bahian religions and the Catholic Church. Catholicism is the majority religion in Brazil, and has been since colonial times. However, the statistics of religious association do not tell the entire story. The people of other faiths include those who practise the Afro-Brazilian religions descended from the former slaves who brought their religious traditions with them from Africa. When the slaves arrived, they were forced to convert to Catholicism, which led to the merging of religions. Today this mixing of different faiths continues.

A popular saying describes Bahians as a practical people who go to church in the morning, a Spiritism session in the afternoon . . . and a Candomblé ritual in the evening. Bahians tend to be eclectic because no one knows for sure, of course, which path is the one that will insure the fulfilment of their needs and wishes. (Silverstein, 1995, p. 137)

In the face of this situation, a definition limited to Catholicism or to Christianity does not fit. The communities within which CEAS works reflect this mixture of faiths.

Alfredo Dorea, Jesuit priest and CEAS staff member, speaking in an interview for a programme on Salvador, Brazil for BBC2, confirmed this integration of Catholicism with other religions, in his experience (*Brazil: Inside Out* [2003]). 'I'd say that here in Brazil the negroes never had a European faith. The faith of our people here, was born like this, already plural. So we bring together a melting of many faith traditions.'[15] The interviewer then asked what his opinion was of a person who may be praying to Mary and also seeing her as Iemanja, the goddess of the sea in Candomblé. In this tradition, the gods and goddesses were overlaid with the Christian saints so that the practice appeared to be Catholic. Today, the saints have double meanings for many people, whether they consider themselves to be Catholic or of another faith. To this question Dorea responded, 'If anyone has faith, it's good they come to the House of God. Whatever faith it is. If you have faith, you're welcome.' This is the multi-faith situation in which CEAS, and Christian Aid too, implement the hermeneutical circle.

Within this situation, the poor remain the starting point for reflection in the hermeneutical circle, in its expanded definition of powerlessness in all its forms.

### *The poor as the starting point for theology*

The 21st Century Christian will opt for those excluded or s/he will not be Christian. While the criminal inequality in the world grows, as well as those human beings, excluded from life and from dignity, the option for the poor becomes more and more an essential component of the Church of Jesus. (Oliveira, 2001, p. 25)[16]

The poor and excluded are central to praxis. Padre Alfredo Dorea conducted a weekly Mass in a cathedral in the centre of Salvador. In his homilies, he focused on relating the Scriptures to the lives of the poorest. In one such homily, discussing Peter walking on water, he said that while

---

15 All of these are the translations used in the documentary.
16 De Oliveira is quoting Dom Pedro Casaldáliga.

walking on water may seem like a miracle, it is not as much of a miracle as the survival of the poorest every day in Brazil.

The poor are the starting point for theology, for knowing God. Theology is revealed through praxis in communities of the poor and excluded, as CEAS's practice shows. They start in the communities of the excluded and challenge the centres of power, as we saw with liberation theology. The powerless call the powerful to build just relationships.[17]

## Sin in structures and between humans in community

How are the relationships between the rich and the poor sinful? Another of the Masses led by Dorea focused on Matthew 19.23–4, Mark 10.25, and Luke 18. 24–5, where Jesus said that it is easier for a camel to go through the eye of a needle than for a rich person to enter heaven. For Dorea, this statement is literally true. In the economic realm, having more separates a person from others around them and makes it harder for all to become part of the community of God. Even something as simple as a new pair of shoes makes a person stand out from someone without shoes, breaking down community.[18] Thus, for CEAS, the prioritization of the poor requires reducing the wealth of the rich. In God's new earth there will be no inequality.

CEAS emphasizes the exploitative relationships in trading communities, as the earlier chapter analysed through Dussel. People have to become aware that there are structures of sin. They have to struggle against them, recognizing the alternatives that can and do exist. In CEAS's case, these alternatives arise in the civic and political realms.

---

17 And, although there is no room to expand further here, they also deal with poverty as race, gender and sex. For those who read Portuguese, see their website www.ceas.com.br or their journal *Cadernos do CEAS*, which often contains articles by staff members and transcripts of their debates, etc.

18 This reflects Luke 3.11, quoted and questioned earlier by a Christian Aid staff member. At Christian Aid, they debated whether the person with two tunics should literally give up the extra one to someone who has none.

Christians are to work toward God's new earth in community where justice will rule.

Beginning in communities of the poor, people can begin to create an alternative, the just new earth.

## Conscientization for the sharing of power in community

It is in this struggle that people discover points that are fundamental: the solidarity and the love of one another. Whoever doesn't have this is not capable of struggle! (Lurdinha in Debate [2001], p. 69)

How will structures and individuals be redeemed? What is the alternative? A just system has a balance of power. This balance does not occur automatically. It requires a process of conscientization in community. This conscientization merges faith and praxis.

This conscientization, however, does not mean that resolving the situation will be simple. While the end point is clear, there still has to be constant action and reflection to encourage communities to move toward the goal and to ensure that power remains decentralized in community. In order for power to be shared in community, several elements have to be in place. As we saw with the concept of true democracy, people have to be able to participate. People have to be working together. All have to show love for each other. There has to be diversity. Finally, the concept of communion is central. It is in the celebration of the Eucharist that a model for community can be found.

## The Eucharist: Model for life in community

Liberation theologians draw on the model of the Eucharist for life in community. The Eucharist shares the body and blood of Christ equally in community. The body is bread. The bread that is used in the Eucharist is produced by human hands and made sacred by God. This contrasts with the situation in reality where not all have equal access to bread.[19]

---

19 Neto, quoting Dom Gílio Felício, Assistant Bishop of the Archdiocese of

The bread of the Eucharist and the bread of daily life are merged just as the theological and the secular have been merged throughout this analysis. The Masses conducted by Dorea and others weekly in a cathedral in the centre of Salvador are attended by over 200 people. The seats and aisles are filled and often there are people standing outside the doors in the street listening to the Mass. In this Mass, the Eucharist is celebrated as in a Western Catholic Mass. However, there is a second celebration toward the end of the Mass. Between 20 and 30 women gather in the back of the church with baskets of bread that they have baked that day. They move up the centre aisle to the front where the priests bless the baskets. These baskets are then passed through the cathedral and each person receives a small loaf of bread, a second sharing of bread in community. This celebration is accompanied by singing and the moving of the priests through the crowd, also blessing the participants. In this way, the Mass ends.

Participation in this community includes every person regardless of race or gender or any other characteristic that causes people to be excluded. This celebration clearly shows that the sacred realm and the secular realm cannot be separated. The same can be said of the Christian community in general. The Christian community is meant to share all with each other because of the love of God and the other. This sharing merges the sacred, the economic, the political, and the social realms.

## Context in the North: Christian Aid

Christian Aid is comfortable with its partners defining their own practice. It supports and funds CEAS's practice. However, in this case, Christian Aid did not reflect the views of CEAS with regard to development and globalization. The final chapter will consider this further.

---

São Salvador, argued that the poor were struggling for their 'daily bread' (*pão de cada dia*) (9). And finding an economic solution, like employment is simply not enough. 'It's no use to speak of teaching to fish when the person doesn't have a rod, the fish-hook doesn't have a worm and the river is polluted' (9).

In addition, where CEAS had no gap between its faith and practice, Christian Aid did. What does this mean for the practice of agencies in the North like Christian Aid? What should they be struggling toward? How can they blend their reflection and practice with that of their partners?

## Conclusion

CEAS differs from Christian Aid in its analysis of the development paradigm and globalization from their location amongst the poorest. Development and globalization, for CEAS, are simply continuations of the destructive policies of colonialism and must be rejected. Instead, CEAS focuses on political and civic structures, emphasizing the importance of developing citizenship in community, rather than consumption, as their communities have no opportunity to consume.

Both CEAS and the communities in which it works follow the hermeneutical circle. Their goal is social transformation for justice, focusing on the poorest communities. They aim to build the capacity of these communities to participate in the political realm. The communities then define their own goals within this context.

This hermeneutical circle merges the spiritual and the secular. The poor are the starting point for faith and praxis. This praxis is to convert structures of sin, which destroy communities. In just community, there will be no rich and poor. The process of conscientization urges the building of just, not dominating (sinful) relationships. The Eucharist is a further model for economic, political, and spiritual life in community.

Finally, although CEAS draws on the tradition of liberation theology, their action and reflection expands beyond Christianity. Their *caminhada* is multifaith. The communities in which CEAS works are also multifaith and their success in merging realms could be instructive for us.

# Part IV

## *What Should We Be Struggling Toward?*

# 7

# A New Heaven and a New Earth

While many of the theologians and practitioners we encountered used similar theological language, they sometimes disagreed in practice. Using the language of a new heaven and a new earth, sin as injustice, salvation as justice, and justice as the struggle toward this new earth led even partners like Christian Aid and CEAS to emphasize different practice. Part of this disagreement stems from the tension between the present and the future in God's new earth. I suggest six areas of tension to be considered further.

1 Development/Advocacy
2 Advocacy/Conscientization (Empowerment)
3 Consumption/Citizenship
4 Faith/Practice
5 Pragmatism/Prophecy
6 Christianity/Faith

Consideration of each of these could illuminate our future action and reflection.

## Development/Advocacy

There is a tension between relief and development work and advocacy work. Relief and development work aims to alleviate the suffering of the most marginalized in the present mainly through funding changes in the South, offering money or various goods from the North to the South. We have seen that development practice is contested.

Advocacy work aims to change the structures and systems that allow the South to suffer in the first place. It is often focused on the North. Development and advocacy are sometimes justified together by the following argument: radical policies will change the structures and systems, introducing the new earth but it will take some time to implement full-scale change. Thus, there is also action that needs to be taken now to alleviate immediate suffering. While this argument is true in part, unfortunately, it has also been used to support relief and development without advocacy. To maintain and deal with this tension requires a careful and considered process of action and reflection, both in the work of alleviating suffering and in advocating structural change.

Within the work to change the structures and systems, there is a spectrum of ideas ranging from reform to complete overhaul. Often, agencies in the South advocate more urgent and far-reaching changes than those in the North, as we saw with CEAS, in part because they are based in communities of the poorest. For agencies like Christian Aid integrating these perspectives is crucial because they state that they advocate on behalf of their partners. Their legitimacy comes from these partners in the UK and overseas. If northern agencies call for reform when their partners in the South call for overhaul, are they prioritizing the excluded?

Further, advocacy enshrines the power of agencies in the North in two respects. First, the North has the money to give to the poorer countries and the North can decide what it is given for. Second, those in the North have the power to (not) call for changes to structures and systems. They have the power to (not) define and address the 'root causes'. Is it their responsibility to use this power wisely or to get rid of this power?

## Advocacy/Conscientization (Empowerment)

This brings to the fore a second tension between conscientization (empowerment) and advocacy. Conscientization is a process occurring within the poorest communities where people gain the knowledge and

power to change their own lives. Advocacy to change the system, in contrast, comes from those who are not poor, acting on behalf of and with those who are poor. The question is one of empowerment, as development practitioners have consistently argued.[1] While the people in power may use their power for good, there is still an inequality in the distribution of power. This inequality will not exist in God's new earth. Thus, as we work toward the new earth, we should work toward ending this inequality. So what action is required?

We can ask whether the 'development' practice and advocacy are encouraging conscientization or whether they are 'harmful', as Dussel argued partial reforms were. And, if the practice and/or advocacy is harmful, should it continue? Can we allow contradictions between the present situation and the future new earth to continue? If capitalism, for example, is 'the worst system' we have 'except for all the others', as Harries argued, should we be working within it? Should we be imagining new systems, new alternatives, and putting these into practice? As the medical oath states, shouldn't we first 'do no harm'?[2]

Both of these tensions arise within and between communities like CEAS, who reject development, and those like Christian Aid, who still work within the development paradigm. Such tensions need to be regularly reflected upon. The balancing of the present and the future in God's new earth is critical.


## Consumption/Citizenship

To move one step further, should we be focused on the economic realm? Should we be focused on citizenship or consumption? And within economics, do we have to focus on the accumulation of money or on economic growth?

---

1 See the work of Freire, Chambers, and Mesters, for example.

2 For example, with regard to debt, can we argue that it is aid, when they pay the banks back several times more than they receive? Which causes more harm: refusing to lend $1 or demanding $9 in return? Are these our only choices?

Economics has been prioritized, elevated above other realms. Power is given over to it. This ideology has been defined as economism,[3] which allows 'economics to dominate society' (Cobb, 1999, p. 1). However, human beings are more than just consumers. Limiting humanity to the marketplace devalues life outside the market. People can and do live outwith the global marketplace.

The difference between treating human beings as full citizens and treating them as consumers is crucial to achieving just community. Those who cannot consume have no say if we prioritize consumption. Prioritizing the citizen, on the other hand, introduces the possibility of participation by all in the building of community.

To regain the balance between a holistic citizenship and consumption, between the realms, certain decisions could be taken that contrast with those presently assumed in the global marketplace. Suggestions include:

1 'to confirm that human life has a greater value than that of the market';
2 'to proclaim the rights of peoples as against the rights of business';
3 'to embrace an ethic and a spirituality which consolidates the solidarity of all human beings, North and South'. (Houtard and Polet, 2001, pp. vii–viii)

These decisions accept that human beings should be the focus of attention, not money. And not just humans, but the environment, the earth. By prioritizing people over the market, the poor can become human again and money can return to a thing. Instead of the rich consuming the poor, all human beings can become human again in the wider system.

This requires a focus on power within structures, not just changes to the attitudes and actions of individuals. Poverty, whether economic, political, or cultural is caused by injustice, the imbalance of power between individuals and within structures. Recalling society to a balance between citizenship and consumption can help to restore these unequal structures of power.

---

3 Cobb contrasts economism with 'earthism', a concept focusing on ecology. For comparison of the two ideas see Cobb, 1999.

For example, in advocacy, one can ask: why do I have this power in the first place? Living in right relation requires a balance of power, not just a benevolent use of power. This balance of power begins in local communities and expands to the global level.

Again, maintaining the tension between the present and future in the new earth means recognizing that people and structures will tend toward accumulating and abusing power because God's new earth is not yet fully here. Sin remains. Thus, people have to work to constantly redistribute power keeping the end goal of the new earth in focus.

Reintroducing a focus on citizens requires further reflection from a theological perspective. For example, Forrester cites Philippians 3.20, 'we are citizens of heaven' (Forrester, 2003a, p. 43). Christians can learn about citizenship in this world from their citizenship in God's kingdom.

Christians are understood to be citizens of God's kingdom, not consumers of the kingdom. This is an important distinction to make as we work toward God's new earth. The work is not an attempt to purchase a place in the new earth. Redemption is not purchased. However, human beings are citizens, active participants, in the struggle.

In the celebration of the Eucharist, power is distributed equally. All who partake of the body and blood are empowered to live out community in God's new earth. The sharing of consumption, power, and participation in community can provide a model for exercising power that is not based on domination in each realm. This does not mean that focusing on human beings as citizens alone would lead to the new earth. There is potential for idolatry in each realm. How can we balance the realms? How can we ensure we are not worshipping idols?

This acceptance of the need for active citizens also does not mean that the Western conception of democracy may be appropriate for every society. Just as with the economic system, there should be heterogeneity, not homogeneity in the solutions proposed, acknowledging the diversity within and between communities. For example,

the decision-making process relies, in many non-European cultures, on consensus. It involves a slow, careful attempt to safeguard the collective harmony, whereas the Western-style of decision-making,

by majority over minority, represents for them a sort of brutality, lastingly harmful to the social body. (Verhelst, 1990, p. 40)

There may be other styles of government where each of the aspects of a true democracy is present from participation to communion.

To find these alternatives, to address other realms, liberation theology can be challenged to return to its roots: to participate in the hermeneutical circle in communities around the world.

## Faith/Practice

The hermeneutical circle needs to be fully implemented and integrated.[4] In order to balance the current work toward a new earth with what God's new earth will finally look like, there has to be constant reflection on this action. This reflection should never be taken as dogma but should lead to further action and reflection, a continuing spiral of the hermeneutical circle. In this way, the spiral moves closer toward the goal of the new earth, not repeating the same mistakes but building on the experience.[5]

The starting point of the hermeneutical circle is one's own place in reality. This simple starting point has been dismissed within the development paradigm and globalization, which assume that all people are on the same path. Each community's starting point depends on their culture. One such starting point begins with relations in community rather than the individual.

At Christian Aid there is a tension between the theological reflection, which tends toward rejection of the development paradigm, and the policy, which works within the development paradigm. Their theologi-

---

4 Petrella, 2006, has an excellent analysis of the hermeneutical circle and the need for a return to 'historical projects' in liberation theology, both of which can be instructive here.

5 This process is difficult for Christian Aid, as it works within the development paradigm, while at the same time, the theologians it reflects on and asks to reflect with its staff, such as Gorringe and Selby, work from themes in liberation.

cal reflection was unclear. Agencies like Christian Aid could contribute to and participate more fully in the hermeneutical circle, strengthening their practice and advocacy. If faith is the basis of their work, which they argue it is, it should not be left to the margins itself. How can agencies link reflection and action without a process in place?

## Pragmatism/Prophecy

Could we perhaps argue that Christian Aid,[6] for example, is prophetic in the praxis it funds but pragmatic with its advocacy? And if so, should there be conflict between the two?[7] Can they both point toward the new heaven and the new earth?

Christian Aid distinguishes between pragmatic and prophetic uses of power. For Dudley, the campaign that urged supermarkets to provide fair trade products, was a pragmatic use of consumer power but it failed to be prophetic because it confirmed people in their roles as consumers. A prophetic approach would challenge the unequal power of consumers because in God's new earth there will be no power inequality. Instead, a pragmatic approach argues for ethical use of that power. Yet, the example of CEAS shows that a community can aim for a balance of power.

The theological discussions at Christian Aid seem to support the prophetic approach over the pragmatic. If the difference between radical positions and the middle ground that Christian Aid advocates is presented as a distinction between prophecy and pragmatism, what is the role of prophecy? 'With the kingdom in mind, we hope we can be both prophetic and pragmatic as we attempt to be faithful' (Dudley, 2002, p. 8). Christian Aid wants to include prophecy and pragmatism in its reflection.

How would the prophetic reflection impact the practice?

---

6 Although my case study is of Christian Aid, I would argue that similar tensions exist within other agencies in the North.

7 Why did Christian Aid focus on trade, when such a focus excluded the world's poorest countries?

As we engage in this aspect of mission, the prophetic tradition nour-
ishes us as we identify injustices that need transformation. We try to be
prophetic because we pray with the ancient prophets that God's name
would be hallowed and God's will can be done on earth as it is in
heaven. (p. 8)

The prophetic aspect is to point to what the world should become.
However, 'we try to be pragmatic because millions of people need
change now' (p. 8). Thus, the pragmatic part is to try to change small
elements within the system now, to relieve the suffering of the poor. At
the same time, one aims toward prophetic changes in the long term, a
mixture of development with advocacy. Yet many, including CEAS, disagree with this mixture, arguing that this pragmatism still works within a
system that worships Mammon and other gods. This system is in conflict
with the long-term changes needed.

One could argue that pragmatism is practical and prophecy is imprac-
tical. Yet, this negates the fact that theological reflection should begin
from the hermeneutical circle, from praxis. Reflection is linked to practice. This theological reflection, in the case of Christian Aid, tends
toward the prophetic, as does the practice of at least one of its partners. A
prophetic approach has practical elements too; it is not merely theoreti-
cal. 'Prophecy is the application of vision to a particular situation'
(Forrester, 2003b, p. 117). There can be (and are) practical local alternatives to engage in, while at the same time urging a complete overhaul of
the system. Rather than trying to set aside the prophecy in favour of a
pragmatic approach, continuing the process of action and reflection
could blur the stark lines between the two.

The tension between where Christian Aid and CEAS are located now
and where they will be located in God's new earth will remain. However,
where CEAS refuses to support sinful structures of power, Christian Aid
works within them, critiquing them. It is here that reflection has to
be allowed to impact action. Christian Aid cannot limit its theological
critique of power to individuals. Its policy already addresses the structures. The theological reflection could follow suit.

What is key is to refuse to allow the pragmatic practice to contradict

the prophetic approach. We do not have to decide between pragmatism and prophecy. Conscientization and advocacy can balance each other, challenging the other to produce ways of practically and prophetically working toward God's new earth.[8] Those working toward pragmatic changes to the systems today need to be aware of how these changes bring us closer to God's new earth.

Within the discussion of charity and justice, charity was not rejected altogether. However, charity was subsumed within the overall consideration of justice. Charity is only needed when a situation of injustice exists. On its own, charity is not enough; it leaves the person 'giving' with the power. It does not ask why they have more to 'give' in the first place. It does not ask how to achieve a just system, where no one holds greater economic, political, racial, gender, or other types of power over another human being. That is the role for advocacy.

A similar distinction can be made between the pragmatic and prophetic approaches toward change. Pragmatism, like charity, can be a useful means of moving the situation forward toward a new earth but only when subsumed within a prophetic discussion. As the charitable act must be located within the larger spectrum of achieving justice, the pragmatic act must be located within the larger spectrum of the prophetic challenge.

The challenge, as with each of these tensions, is to always be pointing toward God's new earth. Within liberation theology, the themes of God's new earth, justice, community, prioritizing the poor, and redeeming structures can all be further developed to consider how to move forward. Yet, such reflection cannot remain solely within Christian theology, if it is to be truly inclusive.

## Christianity/Faith

The final point to be considered in the struggle toward God's new earth is how to expand this struggle beyond Christian communities. This point is particularly relevant for an agency like Christian Aid, which

---

8  This seems to be the case at CEAS.

draws support from diverse communities. Practising the hermeneutical circle in communities of the poorest in the UK and around the world would mean including those outside the churches and in different places of worship. The spirituality of the poor is not limited to the Christian faith or churches.

This new earth encompasses the material as well as spiritual realms. It can be worked toward by those of different faiths and those without faith. Secular development practitioners use spiritual terms like 'repentance' to describe the needed changes. Those of any faith (or of undefined faith) can participate in the hermeneutical circle. This action/reflection process links the spiritual, economic, political and social realms.

> Religious groups have to find in their traditions and in inter-religious dialogue values and attitudes that will permit them to assume in a creative and humanising way the new global economic, social and cultural conditions. (Serrano,[9] 2001, p. 31)

The hermeneutical circle lead to differences among and between communities, which will have to be addressed. However, these differences already exist. What the hermeneutical circle introduces is a means of dealing with difference. It does so by building on the experience of the poor as we struggle together toward God's new earth.

Having begun with the question of what Christians should struggle toward, we end with the challenge of expanding the hermeneutical circle to include the spirituality of the poor in whatever form it may take. The tension between the present and the future incarnations of the new earth will remain, challenging us to reflect on our action in community.

What is the scandal of poverty? How can we eradicate poverty? How can we challenge structures and systems to eradicate poverty too?

---

9 Josep Serrano is an economist, theologian, and member of the Board of *Cristianisme I Justícia*.

# Conclusion

I began the book with a diary excerpt from a meeting of Christian Aid, a faith-based relief and development organization. Using it as a case study I wanted to answer the question: what should Christians be struggling toward – development or liberation? The lack of a theology of development might suggest that the answer is liberation. And, in fact, this is what I believe. But does the lack of a theology of development mean that it cannot exist? And, is it worthwhile to talk of development at all when the word has come to be so misused?

What can Christians work toward? Many people in the North and South agree that faith can be mixed with practice, even if they disagree on what that practice is. Based on the two case studies, and the history I have traced, I argue that the quest for a theology of development should be abandoned, and a theology of liberation should be reinvigorated from the communities on the ground around the world.

CEAS showed that it is possible to merge liberative faith with practice. Each of their interactions suggested further ways for liberation theologians to reflect. CEAS, and liberation theology, speak to us from the underside of history, arguing that it should be the excluded who are at the centre. They should decide what justice means, aiming for a balance of power.

Why do I think that the theologies of development cannot answer the deeper questions the theologies of liberation ask? Because development, as practised, argues that there is one hegemonic economic system that can be rolled out to all corners of the earth. It masks the fact that while the income of some rises and makes countries appear to be wealthier, there

are many within those countries who become poorer: economically, politically, environmentally, sexually, etc. The improvement of a few is used to justify the debasement of the many. If we are to treat others as we treat Christ, we are debasing Christ and therefore, have an unjust relationship with God.

Rejecting development, I argue for liberation: liberation from oppression, including the ideology of economic growth, including any hegemony; liberation to act in the economic, political, environmental, sexual and other realms. This liberation includes empowerment: enabling the poor to free themselves, to act to better their lives. There are changes needed in all of these realms in countries around the world, including the UK and USA.

Development implies the changes are needed in the South alone. This is simply not true. It is true that, although we do have a North–South divide, we also have a powerful–powerless divide that encompasses companies, countries, and communities within and outwith countries around the world. There are many forms of poverty and many forms of domination by the powerful: including economic, political, environmental, sexual and spiritual.

CEAS reflects traditional areas of liberation theology and suggests other areas for reflection, like inter-faith dialogue and the civic realm. It continues work in the areas of economics, politics, sex, race, gender and the environment. Contrary to those who proclaimed the death of liberation theology, faith and praxis continue to be merged.

Development is not salvation. Neither is liberation when tied to a solely material system, as many liberation theologians have argued. We are to work toward God's new earth even though it is not yet fully present. And this is one of the positive aspects of the hermeneutical circle. It allows for action but doesn't enshrine this action. It subjects it to further reflection.

This history began with the question of whether theology could lend advice to development. A theology of development failed. It could not support development. A theology supportive of capitalism had to reconfigure the notion of justice and focus its theology on the rich. This type of theology continues to marginalize those who cannot participate equally

in the dominant group in economic, political, cultural, sexual and religious realms. I believe development should be rejected, until once again, devoid of its connection with economic growth, we can re-explore its original definition of 'evolving and changing'.

A theology of development stagnated and in its place arose a theology of liberation. This theology with its new method, was not constrained. It rejected development. And the global discussion, accepting development, eventually rejected liberation theology, declaring it dead along with the demise of socialism and communism.

However, despite its press, themes of liberation are alive and well. But it has work to do. We need to consider ways to decrease our wealth and poverty, however that poverty be defined. It is still relevant to ask what Christian theology has to say about development. It is also relevant to ask what those experiencing development have to say about theology. (How) can we keep partial reforms from being worthless or harmful?

Development and liberation are indeed opposites, as many development practitioners have realized, as they search for alternatives. We saw development and liberation merged in the practice of Christian Aid and it led to questions and possible conflicts. Christian Aid uses the language of development, yet allows its partners to define, choose and implement their own policies. At least one of their partners rejects the development paradigm altogether.

Although many have co-opted the method and themes of liberation to discuss capitalism and development, the combination is unsuccessful. The emerging Christian themes lead to a rejection of development as economic growth. First, the North cannot remain focused on capitalism as the solution to underdevelopment when underdevelopment is not 'the problem'. There are problems with poverty across the globe, whether defined economically, politically or otherwise.

Second, we should not assume that one hegemonic system needs to be put in place for the entire world, or that we are powerless to act until we find that one system.[1] The call for alternatives merges the spiritual and

---

1 Petrella explores this in his work *The Future of Liberation Theology*.

secular realms.[2] It may be that aspects of capitalism or socialism could be employed locally and it may also be that there is nothing to be served by either system and that new alternatives need to be searched out. Neither capitalism nor democracy can be assumed to be 'the solution' at the outset. That is to end the hermeneutical circle before it begins.

Third, in defining the problem and the solution, we in the North have continued to assume that we have the answers to others' problems. And if these answers benefit us too, so much the better. We need to consider that we (however we hold power) may be the problem and that we too have problems. There is a question not only of increasing the power of the excluded in various realms but of decreasing the power of the elite.

What remains is the need to begin in communities of the poor, in whatever way they are poor. The new heaven and new earth will not be (and are not now) solely economic or political systems. We should be struggling toward a holistic implementation and the parts should not be contrary to the whole, even if we cannot see what that whole might fully be.

We are whole persons. The theologies of liberation – and of development, if it is pursued further – both have work to do and this work should begin not from theory but from the experience of communities on the ground. Let's return to these communities to see what they are doing, what alternatives they have already managed to put in place despite our focus on the hegemonic system.[3] What do they have to say about faith and practice today?[4]

---

2 See, for example, Sidaway's discussion of post-development.

3 I would suggest that as a next step, you could read two books: Petrella's *The Future of Liberation Theology* and Taylor's *Christianity, Poverty and Wealth*. Taylor's book summarizes the contributions of many around the world to those themes and Petrella concisely summarizes the work to be done by liberation theologians. Merging the two together could be extremely useful in communities of the poorest around the world.

4 This work has already begun. See, for example, Althaus-Reid's *The Queer God* and Petrella's *Latin American Liberation Theology: The Next Generation*.

Liberation theology grew out of a critique of repressive governments and economic development. Its merging of themes with post-development and alternatives to development practice is not surprising. Christian Aid, and other development agencies, could move forward from this critique. It could more fully reflect the voices of its partners, even if these voices are in disagreement.

Liberation theology remains relevant as it critiques injustice and suggests models for redeeming sinful structures and individuals: conscientization and praxis in communities of the excluded. The excluded remain the starting point for theology. They call the powerful to repentance. They show us our sinfulness. We need to recognize human beings as citizens, whole human beings, not simply consumers. And, we in the North, the powerful, need to listen and not be content with our theology, or lack thereof, that prioritizes the rich and powerful. We are not safe in the knowledge that God's kingdom has not yet arrived.

We need a hermeneutic of suspicion. We need to examine reality in the light of faith and social science, faith in the light of reality and social science, and social science in the light of faith and reality. This is inter-disciplinarity.

First, there is a step of conscientization for each of us in community. What is our reality? How and why are we poor? How and why do we make others poor? What does this reality have to say about our faith? What does our faith have to say about this reality? What action should we take based on this reflection?

Theology here is not primary, neither are the social sciences. Theory is not primary; action is. Theology is done by all of us; we are all theologians. The same is true of the social sciences. People do not live by theory; theory should explain what happens on the ground. Further, our goal is not dogma, it is a new heaven and a new earth.

Theology is faith seeking an understanding of all forms of poverty through action and reflection. God works in history and so we can see the beginnings of the new heaven and the new earth in this history, as imperfect as they may be. This is why it is critical for our partial pictures of the new heaven and new earth not to be in conflict. We are struggling for justice, the balancing of power that will exist in God's new earth. We

should never be satisfied with the *status quo* because that is not God's new heaven and new earth. We need to continue asking and answering Gutiérrez's question: 'How do we relate the work of building a just society to the absolute value of the kingdom?'

# Bibliography

Abrecht, Paul, 1961, *The Churches and Rapid Social Change*, Garden City: Doubleday & Company.

Abrecht, Paul and Francis, John, eds, 1975, *Facing Up to Nuclear Power*, Edinburgh: Saint Andrew Press.

Abrecht, Paul and Koshy, Ninian, eds, 1984, *Before It's Too Late: The Challenge of Nuclear Disarmanment*, Geneva: WCC.

Adriance, Madeleine Cousineau, 1995, *Promised Land. Base Christian Communities and the Struggle for the Amazon*, New York: State University of New York Press.

Althaus-Reid, Marcella Maria, 2000a, 'Bién Sonados? The Future of Mystical Connections in Liberation Theology', *Political Theology* 3:44–63.

— 2000b, 'Liberation Theology', in *The Oxford Companion to Christian Thought*, eds Adrian Hastings, Alistair Mason and Hugh Pyper, Oxford: Oxford University Press, 387–90.

— 2000c, *Indecent Theology*, London: Routledge.

Bannock, Graham, Baxter, R. E. and Davis, Evan, eds, 1992, *The Penguin Dictionary of Economics*, London: Penguin Books.

Batstone, David, Mendieta, Eduardo, Lorentzen, Lois Ann and Hopkins, Dwight, eds, 1997, *Liberation Theologies, Postmodernity, and the Americas*, London: Routledge.

Bauer, Gerhard, 1970, *Towards a Theology of Development. An Annotated Bibliography Compiled by Gerhard Bauer for Sodepax*, Geneva: WCC.

Bennett, John C., ed., 1966, *Christian Social Ethics in a Changing World, an Ecumenical Inquiry*, The Church and Society, London: SCM Press.

Boesak, Allan, 1976, *Farewell to Innocence: A Socio-Ethical Study on Black Theology and Black Power*, Maryknoll: Orbis Books.

Boff, Clodovis, 1987, *Theology and Praxis: Epistemological Foundations*,

translated by Robert R. Barr, Maryknoll: Orbis Books.

Boff, Leonardo, 1978, *Jesus Christ Liberator: A Critical Christology of Our Time*, Maryknoll: Orbis Books.

— 1984, *Church, Charism and Power: Liberation Theology and the Institutional Church*, London: SCM Press.

— 1995, *Ecology and Liberation: A New Paradigm*, Ecology and Justice, an Orbis Series on Global Ecology, translated by John Cumming, Maryknoll: Orbis Books.

Boff, Leonardo and Boff, Clodovis, 1987, *Introducing Liberation Theology*, 1. Liberation and Theology, translated by Paul Burns, Tunbridge Wells: Burns & Oates.

Bonino, José Miguez, 1983, *Toward a Christian Political Ethics*, London: SCM Press.

The Brazil Programme – Christian Aid. Latin America and Caribbean Team, London: Christian Aid.

*Brazil: Inside Out.* Programme One, 2003, produced and directed by Per-Eric Hawthorne, BBC, made in association with YLE Finland, videocassette.

Brown, Diana, 1986, *Umbanda: Religion and Politics in Urban Brazil*, Ann Arbor: UMI Research Press.

Burdick, John, 2004, *Legacies of Liberation: The Progressive Catholic Church in Brazil*, Aldershot: Ashgate.

Camara, Helder, 1969, *Church and Colonialism*, London: Sheed & Ward.

Cardenal, Ernesto, 1975, *The Gospel in Solentiname (Vol 2)*, Maryknoll: Orbis Books.

Cardoso, Fernando, 1973, 'The Industrial Elite in Latin America', in *UnderDevelopment and Development: The Third World Today*, ed. Henry Bernstein, Harmondsworth: Penguin Books, 191–204.

CEAS, 1998, A. Equipe Urbana, excerpt from 1998 Report, 3–23, Salvador: CEAS.

— 1999a, Proposta do Termo de Referencia de Avaliacao, Salvador: CEAS.

— 1999b, Relatório de Atividades do CEAS, Periodo: Segundo Semestre 1999, Salvador: CEAS.

— 2000, 'Editorial: Fazenda Brasil', *Cadernos do CEAS* 190:5–13.

— 2001a., 'Análise de Conjuntura: A Importância de Construir a Diferença: As Semelhanças Não se Dão por Acaso', *Cadernos do CEAS* 192:11–26.

— 2001b, 'Análise de Conjuntura: Rumo a 2002: Nem CPI, Nem Cassação', *Cadernos do CEAS* 194:9–19.

— 2001c, 'Editorial: Ano Um', *Cadernos do CEAS* 191:5–9.

— 2001d, 'Editorial: Eles Passarão', *Cadernos do CEAS* 193:5–8.

— 2001e, 'Editorial: Ode ao Ser da Classe Média', *Cadernos do CEAS* 194:5–8.

— 2001f, 'Editorial: Vida, Sim; Dependência, Não!', *Cadernos do CEAS* 192:5–9.

— 2001g, Ampliada de Monitoria – 08.08.01, 9.30–16h. Linha II: Organização Popular no Neio Urbano. Salvador: CEAS.

— 2001h, Avaliação do I Semestre de 2001: Linha 2 – Organização e Educação Popular no Meio Urbano. Salvador: CEAS.

— 2001i, Coordenação: Relatório de Reunião: 01.08.01, Minutes, Salvador: CEAS.

— 2001j, Equipe Urbana: Linha Programática II/Organização e Educação Popular no Meio Urbano: Relatório Semestral de Atividades, ano: julho de 2001, Salvador: CEAS.

— 2001k, Oficina de Educação Popular Paulo Freire, Salvador: CEAS.

— 2001l, Planejamento 2001, Salvador: CEAS.

— 2001m, Projeto Christian Aid 2001, Salvador: CEAS.

— 2001n, Relatório Annual. Período: Janeiro a dezembro de 2001, Salvador: CEAS.

— 2001o, Relatório Reunião Coordenação: 22.08.01, Minutes, Salvador: CEAS.

— 2001p, Reunião Coordenação: 28.03.01, Minutes, Salvador: CEAS.

— 2001q. Reunião Coordeenação CEAS: 19/09/01, Minutes, Salvador: CEAS.

— 2001r, Reunião da Coordenação: 18.04.01, Minutes, Salvador: CEAS.

— 2001s, Reunião da Coordenação: 25.04.01, Minutes, Salvador: CEAS.

— 2001t, Reunião da Coordenação: 18.07.01, Minutes, Salvador: CEAS.

— 2001u, Reunião da Coordenação: 29.08.01, Minutes, Salvador: CEAS.

— 2001v, Reunião da Coordenação do CEAS: 15/08/01, Minutes, Salvador: CEAS.

— 2002, 'Editorial: Eleições e Nordeste: Novo Discurso, Velhos Ingredientes', *Cadernos do CEAS* 201:5–9.

Chambers, Robert, 1983, *Rural Development: Putting the Last First*, Harlow: Addison Wesley Longman Limited.

— 1997, *Whose Reality Counts? Putting the First Last*, London: Intermediate Technology Publications.

Christian Aid, 1995, All Shall Be Included . . . In the Feast of Life. A 50th birthday statement adopted by the Board of Christian Aid, London: Christian Aid.

— 1998, *Proclaim Liberty: Reflections on Theology and Debt*, London: Christian Aid.

— 1999a, *Life or Debt: Christian Aid Week 1999 Order of Service*, London: Christian Aid.

— 1999b, *Taking Stock: How the Supermarkets Stack Up on Ethical Trading*, London: Christian Aid.

— 1999c, In Step with the Poor, draft, London: Christian Aid.

— 2000a, *Towards a New Earth*, London: Christian Aid.

— 2000b, Christian Aid Corporate Plan 2000-2004, London: Christian Aid.

— 2001a, *The Global Challenge: Christian Aid's Annual Report, An In-depth Look at 2000/2001*, London: Christian Aid.

— 2001b, *Master or Servant? How Global Trade Can Work to the Benefit of Poor People*, London: Christian Aid.

— 2001c, *Trade for Life: I Want to Change International Trade Rules Because . . .*, London: Christian Aid.

— 2001d, *Trade for Life: Questions and Answers*, preliminary version, London: Christian Aid.

— 2002a, *What Does the Lord Require of You? To Act Justly . . .* Six sessions for cells or small groups to help Christians think and act biblically on world issues, London: Christian Aid.

— 2002b, *Whatever You Do for the Least of These, You Do for Me*, leaflet, London: Christian Aid.

— 2003, *Towards a Christian Aid Strategic Framework 2005-2009*, London: Christian Aid.

Christian Aid Latin America and Caribbean Team, 2000, 'CEAS', London: Christian Aid.

Cobb, John B., Jr, 1994, *Sustaining the Common Good: A Christian Perspective on the Global Economy*, Cleveland: The Pilgrim Press.

— 1995, *Is it Too Late?: A Theology of Ecology*, revised edition, London: Denton: Environmental Ethics Books.

— 1999, *The Earthist Challenge to Economism: A Theological Critique of the World Bank*, London: Macmillan Press.

Commission on Theological Concerns of the Christian Conference of Asia, ed., 1981, *Minjung Theology: People as the Subjects of History*, London: Zed Books.

Cone, James H., 1988, *Black Theology of Liberation*, Maryknoll: Orbis Books.

Consultation on Theology and Development, 1970, *In Search of a Theology of Development: Papers from a Consultation Held by Sodepax in Cartigny*

*Switzerland, November 1969*, Geneva: WCC.

Costa, Iraneildson Santos, 2002, "'E Ressuscitou ao Terceiro Milênio . . .":
Em Defesa da Classe como Categoria Básica de Análise', *Cadernos do CEAS*
198:61-80.

Cox, Harvey, 1967, 'Introduction', in Cox, H., ed., *The Church Amid
Revolution*, New York: Association Press, 17-24.

— 1988, *The Silencing of Leonardo Boff: The Vatican and the Future of World
Christianity*, London: Collins.

Croatto, José Severino, 1963-1986, *Exodus: A Hermeneutics of Freedom*,
Maryknoll: Orbis Books.

Cunha, Joaci de Souza, 2001, 'O Prisioneiro, O Censor e a Revolução: Uma
Crítica à Estratégia Socialista em Gramsci', *Cadernos do CEAS* 193:9-32.

— 2003, 'A Dominação do Imperialismo na Bahia', *Cadernos do CEAS*
203:25-50.

Curtis, Mark, 2001, *Trade for Life: Making Trade Work for Poor People*,
London: Christian Aid.

Daly, Herman, 1996, 'Sustainable Growth? No Thank You', in *The Case
Against the Global Economy and For a Turn Toward the Local*, eds. Jerry
Mander and Edward Goldsmith, San Francisco: Sierra Club Books, 192-6.

'Debate: A Luta pela Transformação da Sociedade', [2001] *Cadernos do CEAS*
194:65-90.

Drewry, Martin, Macmullan, Justin and Bentall, Judith, 2002, *Trade Justice: A
Campaign Handbook*, London: Christian Aid.

Drimmelen, Rob van, 1998, *Faith in a Global Economy: A Primer for
Christians*, Geneva: WCC.

Duchrow, Ulrich, 1995, *Alternatives to Global Capitalism: Drawn from Biblical History, Designed for Political Action*, Utrecht: International Books.

Dudley, Rebecca, 2000a, Priming the Pump: Trade for Life, draft, London:
Christian Aid.

— 2000b, We Believe in . . . Life Which Is Life Indeed: Campaigning in Faith
with Christian Aid, workshop briefing paper, London: Christian Aid.

— 2000c, 'We Have a Vision of a New Earth': Theology and the Trade
Campaign, draft: 14 November, London: Christian Aid.

— 2001a, 'We Have a Vision of a New Earth': Theology and the Trade
Campaign, draft: 16 February, London: Christian Aid.

— 2001b, *Trade for Life: Worship and Study Guide. Ideas to Link Prayer and
Action*, London: Christian Aid.

— 2002, Trade for Life: Faith Foundations for Campaigns and Campaigners', draft for Comments, London: Christian Aid.

— 2003a, 'Criticising Economies with Biblical Measures', in *Turn the Tables: Reflections on Faith and Trade*, eds. Rebecca Dudley and Linda Jones, London: CAFOD, 60–64.

— 2003b, 'Foreword', in *Turn the Tables: Reflections on Faith and Trade*, eds. Rebecca Dudley and Linda Jones, 1–2, London: CAFOD.

Dudley, Rebecca and Graystone, Peter, 2000, *For Love or Money: A Christian Aid Lent Course*, London: Christian Aid.

Dudley, Rebecca and Jones, Linda, eds, 2003, *Turn the Tables: Reflections on Faith and Trade*, London: CAFOD.

Dussel, Enrique, 1980, *Philosophy of Liberation*, translated by Aquilina Martinez and Christine Morkovsky, Maryknoll: Orbis Books.

— 1981, *A History of the Church in Latin America: Colonialism to Liberation*, Grand Rapids: William B. Eerdmans Publishing Company.

— 1988, *Ethics and Community*, translated by Robert R. Barr, Theology and Liberation Series, Maryknoll: Orbis Books.

— ed., 1992, *The Church in Latin America: 1492–1992*, Tunbridge Wells: Burns & Oates.

Eakin, Marshall C., 1997, *Brazil: The Once and Future Country*, New York: St Martin's Press.

Edelman, Marc and Haugerud, Angelique, eds, 2005, *The Anthropology of Development and Globalization: From Classical Political Economy to Contemporary Neoliberalism*, Oxford: Blackwell Publishing.

Elliott, Charles, 1966, 'Ethical Issues in the Dynamics of Economic Development', in *Economic Growth in World Perspective*, ed. Denis Munby, The Church and Society, London: SCM Press, 331–67.

— 1971, *The Development Debate*, London: SCM Press.

— 1987, *Comfortable Compassion? Poverty, Power and the Church*, London: Hodder & Stoughton.

Finn, Daniel, 1996, *Just Trading: On the Ethics and Economics of International Trade*, Nashville: Abingdon Press.

Forrester, Duncan, 1988, *Theology and Politics*, Oxford: Blackwell.

— 1989, *Beliefs, Values and Policies*, Oxford: Clarendon.

— 2001a, *On Human Worth: A Christian Vindication of Equality*, London: SCM Press.

— 2001b, 'Social Justice and Welfare', in *The Cambridge Companion to*

*Christian Ethics*, ed. Robin Gill, Cambridge Companions to Religion, Cambridge: Cambridge University Press, 195-208.

— 2003a, 'Citizens of Heaven', in *Turn the Tables: Reflections on Faith and Trade*, eds. Rebecca Dudley and Linda Jones, London: CAFOD, 39-47.

— 2003b, 'The Political Service of Theology in Scotland', in *God in Society: Doing Social Theology in Scotland Today*, eds. William Storrar and Peter Donald, Edinburgh: Saint Andrew Press, 83-121.

Frank, Andre Gunders, 1969, *Capitalism and Underdevelopment in Latin America*, New York: Monthly Review Press.

Freire, Paulo, 1970, *Pedagogy of the Oppressed*, translated by Myra Bergman Ramos, New York: Herder & Herder.

— 1984a, 'Education, Liberation and the Church', *Religious Education*, 79:4, 524-45.

— 1984b, 'Know, Practice, and Teach the Gospels', *Religious Education*, 79:4, 547-8.

— 1985, *The Politics of Education: Culture, Power, and Liberation*, translated by Donaldo Macedo, with an introduction by Henry A Giroux, London: Macmillan Publishers Ltd.

— 1992, *Pedagogy of The City*, New York: The Continuum Publishing Company.

— 1993, *Pedagogy of Hope: Reliving Pedagogy of the Oppressed*, New York: The Continuum Publishing Company.

Freire, Paulo and Shor, Ira, 1987, *A Pedagogy of Liberation*, Basingstoke: Palgrave Macmillan.


Gamboa De Baixo, 2000, Latin America and Caribbean Team, London: Christian Aid.

Gay, Robert, 1999, 'The Broker and the Thief: A Parable (Reflections on Popular Politics in Brazil)', *Luso-Brazilian Review* 36:49-70.

'God and the Global Economy', 2000, workshop flier, Oxford: Christian Aid.

Goertzel, Ted, 1999, *Fernando Henrique Cardoso: Reinventing Democracy in Brazil*, London: Lynne Rienner Publishers.

Goodland, Robert, 1996, 'Growth Has Reached Its Limit', in *The Case Against the Global Economy and For a Turn Toward the Local*, eds. Jerry Mander and Edward Goldsmith, San Francisco: Sierra Club Books, 207-17.

Gorringe, Timothy J., 1994, *Capital and the Kingdom: Theological Ethics and Economic Order*, Maryknoll: Orbis Books.

— 1996, *God's Just Vengeance: Crime, Violence and the Rhetoric of Salvation*, Cambridge: Cambridge University Press.

— 1997, *The Sign of Love: Reflections on the Eucharist*, London: SPCK.

— 1998, 'Political Readings of Scripture', in *The Cambridge Companion to Biblical Interpretation*, ed. John Barton, Cambridge Companions to Religion, Cambridge: Cambridge University Press, 67–80.

— 1999, *Fair Shares: Ethics and the Global Economy*, London: Thames & Hudson.

— 2000a, *Salvation*, Peterborough: Epworth Press.

— 2000b, 'The Shape of the Human Home: Cities, Global Capital and Ec-Clesia', *Political Theology* 3:80–94.

— 2001, 'Liberation Ethics', in *The Cambridge Companion to Christian Ethics*, ed. Robin Gill, Cambridge Companions to Religion. Cambridge: Cambridge University Press, 125–37.

Graystone, Peter, 2000, Personal Communication, 20 September.

Green, Duncan and Melamed, Claire, 2000, *A Human Development Approach to Globalisation*, London: Christian Aid.

Greenbelt service. [2000] London: Christian Aid.

Grey, Mary, 1993, *From Cultures of Silence to Cosmic-Justice-Making: A Way Forward for Theology?* Southampton: University of Southampton.

— 1997, *Beyond the Dark Night: A Way Forward for the Church?* London: Cassell.

— 2000, 'The Shape of the Human Home – A Response to Professor T. Gorringe', *Political Theology* 3:95–103.

— 2002, 'The Gospel of Liberation', in *Colloquium 2000: Faith Communities and Social Movements Facing Globalization*, ed. Ulrich Duchrow, Studies from the World Alliance of Reformed Churches, 45. Geneva: World Alliance of Reformed Churches, 79–84.

Goudzwaard, Bob, 1997, *Capitalism and Progress: A Diagnosis of Western Society*, London: Send the Light Inc.

Guimarães, José Ribeiro Soares, 2001, 'Trabalho, Rendimento e Desigualdades Regionais', *Cadernos do CEAS* 191:21–35.

Gutiérrez, Gustavo, 1974, *A Theology of Liberation: History, Politics and Salvation*, translated by Sister Caridad Inda and John Eagleson, London: SCM Press.

— 1999, 'The Task and Content of Liberation Theology', in *The Cambridge Companion to Liberation Theology*, ed. Christopher Rowland, translated by Judith Connor, Cambridge: Cambridge University Press, 19–38.

Hallman, David, ed., 1994, *Ecotheology: Voices from South and North*, Geneva: WCC.

Harries, Richard, 1992, *Is There a Gospel for the Rich? The Christian in a Capitalist World*, London: Mowbray.

Hauerwas, Stanley, 1991, *Peaceable Kingdom*, Notre Dame: University of Notre Dame Press.

Hines, Colin, 2000, *Localization: A Global Manifesto*, London: Earthscan Publications.

Hinkelammert, Franz J., 1986, *The Ideological Weapons of Death: A Theological Critique of Capitalism*, with an Introduction by Pablo Richard and Raul Vidales, translated by Phillip Berryman, Maryknoll: Orbis Books.

— 1997, 'Liberation Theology in the Economic and Social Context of Latin America: Economy and Theology, or the Irrationality of the Rationalized', in *Liberation Theologies, Postmodernity, and the Americas*, eds. David Batstone, Eduardo Mendieta, Lois Ann Lorentzen, and Dwight N. Hopkins, London: Routledge, 25–52.

Horsley, Richard A., 1996, *Archaeology, History and Society in Galilee: The Social Context of Jesus and the Rabbis*, Valley Forge, Pennsylvania: Trinity Press International.

— ed., 1997, *Paul and Empire: Religion and Power in Roman Imperial Society*, Harrisburg: Trinity Press International.

Houtart, François and Polet, François, eds, 2001, *The Other Davos: the Globalization of Resistance to the World Economic System*, London: Zed Books.

Illich, Ivan, 1992, 'Needs', in *The Development Dictionary: A Guide to Knowledge as Power*, ed. Wolfgang Sachs, London: Zed Books, 88–101.

Kay, Cristobal, 1990, *Latin American Theories of Development and Underdevelopment*, London: Routledge.

Kee, Alistair, ed., 1974, *A Reader in Political Theology*, London: SCM Press.

— 1986, *Domination or Liberation: The Place of Religion in Social Conflict*, London: SCM Press.

— 1990, *Marx and the Failure of Liberation Theology*, London: SCM Press.

— 2000, 'The Conservatism of Liberation Theology: Four Questions for Jon Sobrino', *Political Theology* 3:30–43.

Keen, Steve, 2001, *Debunking Economics: The Naked Emperor of the Social Sciences*, London: Zed Books.

Korten, David, 1990, *Getting to the 21st Century: Voluntary Action and the Global Agenda*, West Hartford: Kumarian Press.

— 1996, 'The Mythic Victory of Market Capitalism', in *The Case Against the Global Economy and For a Turn Toward the Local*, eds. Jerry Mander and Edward Goldsmith, San Francisco: Sierra Club Books, 183–191.

— 1999, *The Post-corporate World: Life after Capitalism*, West Hartford: Kumarian Press.

— 2001, *When Corporations Rule The World*, 2nd edn, Bloomfield: Kumarian Press.

— 2002, 'From Empire to Community: Living the Future into Being', *Development* 45:28–31.

Kothari, Uma, ed., 2005, *A Radical History of Development Studies: Individuals, Institutions and Ideologies*, London: Zed Books.

Koyama, Kosuke, 1977, *No Handle on the Cross*, Maryknoll: Orbis Books.

Kraay, Hendrik, ed., 1998, *Afro-Brazilian Culture and Politics: Bahia, 1790s to 1990s*, London: M. E. Sharpe.

Kuin, Pieter, 1966, 'Economic Growth and Welfare in the Industrialized West', in Denis Munby, ed., *Economic Growth in World Perspective*, New York/London: Association Press/SCM Press, 31–59.


Lang, Tim and Hines, Colin, 1993, *The New Protectionism: Protecting the Future against Free Trade*, London: Earthscan Publications.

Linden, Ian, 2000, 'Liberation Theology: Coming of Age?', *Political Theology* 3:11–29.

Lebret, Louis Joseph, 1965, *The Last Revolution: The Destiny of Over and Underdeveloped Nations*, New York: Sheed & Ward.

Long, Stephen D., 2000, *Divine Economy: Theology and the Market*, London: Routledge.


MacIntyre, Alasdair, 1999, *Dependent Rational Animals: Why Human Beings Need the Virtues*, London: Duckworth.

Madeley, John, ed., 1999, *Trade and the Hungry: How International Trade is Causing Hunger*, Brussels: APRODEV (Association of WCC-related Development Organisations in Europe).

Maimela, Simon, 1994, 'A Black Theology of Liberation', in *Paths of African Theology*, ed. Rosino Gibellini, Maryknoll: Orbis Books.

Mainwaring, Scott P., 1999, *Rethinking Party Systems in the Third Wave of Democratization: The Case of Brazil*, Stanford: Stanford University Press.

Makhijani, Arjun, 1992, *From Global Capitalism to Economic Justice: An Inquiry into the Elimination of Systemic Poverty, Violence and Environmental Destruction in the World Economy*, London: The Apex Press.

— 2004, *Manifesto for Global Democracy*, London: The Apex Press.

Marrs, Cliff, 2002, 'Globalization: A Short Introduction to the New World Religion', *Political Theology* 4:91–116.

Matthews, Z. K., ed., 1966, *Responsible Government in a Revolutionary Age*, The Church and Society, London: SCM Press.

McIntosh, Alistair, 2001, *Soil and Soul: People versus Corporate Power*, London: Aurum Press.

Meeks, Douglas M., 1989, *God the Economist: The Doctrine of God and Political Economy*, Minneapolis: Fortress Press.

Melamed, Claire, 2001, Eliminating World Poverty: Making Globalisation Work for the Poor. UK Government White Paper, December 2000. Summary and Comment, London: Christian Aid.

— 2002a, *What Works? Trade, Policy and Development*, London: Christian Aid.

— 2002b, Personal Communication.

Melamed, Claire and MacMullan, Justin, 2000, Why Campaign on Trade? A Draft Rationale Paper for the Trade Campaign, London: Christian Aid.

Mesters, Carlos, 1993, 'The Use of the Bible in Christian Communities of the Common People', in *The Bible and Liberation: Political and Social Hermeneutics*, revised edn, an Orbis Series in Biblical Studies, eds. Norman K. Gottwald and Richard A. Horsle, Maryknoll: Orbis Booksy, 3–16.

Miranda, José Porfirio, 1977, *Marx and the Bible: A Critique of the Philosophy of Oppression*, translated by John Eagleson, London: SCM Press.

Morgan, Robin, 1977, *Going Too Far*, London: Random House.

Mosley, Paul, 1991, 'Structural Adjustment: A General Overview 1980–89', in *Current Issues in Development Economics*, ed. V. Balasubramaniam and S. Lall, London: MacMillan.

Muelder, Walter G., 1966, 'Theology and Social Science', in John C. Bennett, ed., *Christian Social Ethics in a Changing World, an Ecumenical Inquiry*, The Church and Society, London: SCM Press, 330–47.

Mukarji, Daleep, 2000, *An Introduction to Christian Aid*, London: Christian Aid.

Munby, Denis, ed., 1966, *Economic Growth in World Perspective*, The Church and Society, London: SCM Press.

Nagle, Robin, 1997, *Claiming the Virgin: The Broken Promise of Liberation Theology in Brazil*, London: Routledge.

Nandy, Ashis, 1992, 'State', in *The Development Dictionary: A Guide to Knowledge as Power*, ed. Wolfgang Sachs, London: Zed Books, 264–74.

National Conference of Catholic Bishops, 1986, *Economic Justice for All: Pastoral Letter on Catholic Social Teaching and the U. S. Economy*, Washington: United States Catholic Conference.

Neto, Joviniano Soares de Carvalho, 2001, 'Desafios da Ação Social – Do Local ao Nacional', *Cadernos do CEAS* 196: 9–18.

Nickoloff, James B., ed., 1996, *Gustavo Gutiérrez Essential Writings*, London: SCM Press.

Ninan, George Bishop, 2000, 'Campaign and Theology – A Perspective from a Christian Aid Overseas Partner', Christian Aid Staff Conference, 11–12 September, Swanwick.

Nissiotis, Nikos A., 1971, 'Introduction to a Christological Phenomenology of Development', in *Technology and Social Justice*, ed. Ronald Preston, Valley Forge: Judson Press, 146–60.

Northcott, Michael, 1999, *Life after Debt: Christianity and Global Justice*, London: SPCK.

Novak, Michael, 1982, *The Spirit of Democratic Capitalism*, New York: Simon & Schuster.

— 1986, *Will It Liberate? Questions about Liberation Theology*, New York: Paulist Press.

— 1995, 'Toward a Theology of the Corporation', in *On Moral Business: Classical and Contemporary Resources for Ethics in Economic Life*, eds. Max L. Stackhouse, Dennis P. McCann, and Shirley J. Roels, with Preston N. Williams, Grand Rapids: William B. Eerdmans, 775–85.

Oliveira, Luiz Paulo Jesus de, 2001, 'As Comunidades Eclesiais de Base e os Seus Cantos: Expressões da Realidade e Visões de Mundo', *Cadernos do CEAS* 196:19–40.

Ottmann, Goetz, 2002, *Lost for Words?: Brazillian Liberationism in the 1990s*, Pittsburgh: University of Pittsburgh Press.

Patomaki, Heikki, 2001, *Democratising Globalisation: The Leverage of the Tobin Tax*, London: Zed Books.

Paul VI, 1967, *On The Development of Peoples*, Vatican City: Vatican Polyglot Press.

Petrella, Ivan, ed., 2005, *Latin American Liberation Theology: The Next Generation*, Maryknoll: Orbis Press.

— 2006, *The Future of Liberation Theology: An Argument and Manifesto*, London: SCM Press.

Pieris, Aloysius, 1988, *An Asian Theology of Liberation*, Maryknoll: Orbis Books.

Prebisch, Raul, 1950, *The Economic Development of Latin America and Its Principle Problems*, New York: United Nations.

Preston, Ronald, 1966, 'Christians and Economic Growth', in *Economic Growth in World Perspective*, ed. Denis Munby, The Church and Society, London: SCM Press, 101–23.

— ed., 1971, *Technology and Social Justice*, Valley Forge: Judson Press.

— 1991, *Religion and the Ambiguities of Capitalism: Have Christians Sufficient Understanding of Modern Economic Realities?* London: SCM Press.


Rahnema, Majid, 1992, 'Poverty', in Wolfgang Sachs, ed., *The Development Dictionary, a Guide to Knowledge as Power*, London/New Jersey: Zed Books Ltd, 158–76.

Rahnema, Majid and Bawtree, Victoria, eds, 1997, *The Post-development Reader*, London: Zed Books.

Ramsey, Paul, 1967, *Who Speaks for the Church?*, New York: Abingdon Press.

Redclift, Michael, 1987, *Sustainable Development*, London: Routledge.

Richter, Judith, 2001, *Holding Corporations Accountable: Corporate Conduct, International Codes, and Citizen Action*, London: Zed Books.

Rieger, Joerg, ed., 1998, *Liberating the Future: God, Mammon and Theology*, Minneapolis: Augsburg Fortress.

Rist, Gilbert, 1997, *The History of Development: From Western Origins to Global Faith*, translated by Patrick Camiller, London: Zed Books.

Ruether, Rosemary, 1994, *Gaia and God: An Ecofeminist Theology of Earth Healing*, San Francisco: HarperSanFrancisco.


Santa Ana, Julio de, 1977, *Good News to the Poor: The Challenge of the Poor in the History of the Church*, Geneva: WCC Publications.

— 1978, *Separation Without Hope?: Essays on the Relation between the Church and the Poor during the Industrial Revolution and the Western Colonial Expansion*, Geneva: WCC Publications.

— 1979, *Towards a Church of the Poor: The Work of an Ecumenical Group on the Church and the Poor*, Geneva: WCC Publications.

— 1998, *Sustainability and Globalization*, Geneva: WCC Publications.

Sardar, Ziauddin, 1998, *Postmodernism and the Other: The New Imperialism of Western Culture*, London: Pluto Press.

Savramis, Demosthenes, 1971, 'Theology and Society: Ten Hypotheses', in R. Preston, ed., *Technology and Social Justice*, Valley Forge: Judson Press, 298–421.

Schuurman, Frans, ed., 1993, *Beyond The Impasse: New Directions in Development Theory*, London: Zed Press.

Scottish Christian Aid Committee, 1999, Minutes of the Meeting on Thursday, 4th November, at 41 George IV Bridge, Edinburgh, Edinburgh: Christian Aid.

Scott, Peter and Cavanaugh, William, eds, 2004, *The Blackwell Companion To Political Theology*, Oxford: Blackwell.

Sedgwick, Peter H., 1999, *The Market Economy and Christian Ethics*, Cambridge: Cambridge University Press.

Segundo, Juan Luis, 1977, *Liberation of Theology*, translated by John Drury, Dublin: Gill & Macmillan.

— 1980, 'Capitalism versus Socialism: Crux Theologica', in *Frontiers of Theology in Latin America*, ed. Rosino Gibellini, Maryknoll: Orbis Books, 240–59.

Selby, Peter, 1997, *Grace and Mortgage: The Language of Faith and the Debt of the World*, London: Darton, Longman & Todd.

— 1998, 'Faith Issues and the Debt Debate: One Person's Journey', in *Proclaim Liberty: Reflections on Theology and Debt*, London: Christian Aid, 73–8.

Serrano, Josep F. Maria i, 2001, *Globalisation*, Cristianisme i Justicia Booklets.

Shiva, Vandana and Holla-Bhar, Radha, 1996, 'Piracy by Patent: The Case of the Neem Tree', in *The Case Against the Global Economy and For a Turn Toward the Local*, eds. Jerry Mander and Edward Goldsmith, San Francisco: Sierra Club Books, 146–59.

Sherman, Amy L., 1997, *The Soul of Development: Biblical Christianity and Economic Transformation in Guatemala*, Oxford: Oxford University Press.

Sidaway, James, 2002, 'Post-Development', in *The Companion to Development Studies*, eds. Vandana Desai and Robert B. Potter, London: Arnold, 16–19.

Silverstein, Leni M., 1995, 'The Celebration of Our Lord of the Good End:

Changing State, Church and Afro-Brazilian Relations in Bahia', in *The Brazilian Puzzle: Culture on the Borderlands of the Western World*, eds. David J. Hess and Robert A. Damatta. New York: Columbia University Press, 134–51.

Singh, Kavaljit, 2000, *Taming Global Financial Flows: Challenges and Alternatives in the Era of Financial Globalization. A Citizen's Guide*, London: Zed Books.

Smith, Adam, 1776, *Wealth of Nations*, London: Dent & Sons.

Smith, Christian, 1991, *The Emergence of Liberation Theology: Radical Religion and Social Movement Theory*, London: University of Chicago Press.

Sobrino, Jon, 1978, *Christology at the Crossroads: A Latin American View*, London: SCM Press.

— 1996, 'Central Position of the Reign of God in Liberation Theology', in *Systematic Theology: Perspectives from Liberation Theology*, eds. Jon Sobrino and Ignacio Ellacuría, translated by Robert Barr, London: SCM Press, 38–74.

Soros, George, 1998, *The Crisis of Global Capitalism: Open Society Endangered*, London: Little, Brown and Company.

Stackhouse, Max L., 2000, 'General Introduction', in *Religion and the Powers of the Common Life*, ed. Max L. Stackhouse with Peter J. Paris, *God and Globalization*, Volume 1, Harrisburg: Trinity Press International, 1–52.

Stackhouse, Max L. and McCann, Dennis P., 1995, 'A Postcommunist Manifesto: Public Theology after the Collapse of Socialism', in *On Moral Business: Classical and Contemporary Resources for Ethics in Economic Life*, eds. Max L. Stackhouse, Dennis P. McCann, and Shirley J. Roels, with Preston N. Williams, Grand Rapids: William B. Eerdmans, 949–54.

Stackhouse, Max L. with Paris, Peter J., eds, 2000, *Religion and the Powers of the Common Life. God and Globalization*, Volume 1. Harrisburg: Trinity Press International.

Stackhouse, Max L., Browning, Don S. and Paris, Peter J., eds, 2001, *The Spirit and the Modern Authorities. God and Globalization*, Volume 2. Harrisburg: Trinity Press International.

Stackhouse, Max L. and Obenchain, Diane B., eds, 2002, *Christ and the Dominions of Civilization. God and Globalization*, Volume 3, Harrisburg: Trinity Press International.

Stackhouse, Max L., McCann, Dennis P. and Roels, Shirley J. with Williams, Preston N., eds, 1995, *On Moral Business: Classical and Contemporary*

*Resources for Ethics in Economic Life*, Grand Rapids: William B. Eerdmans.

Starr, Amory, 2000, *Naming the Enemy: Anti-Corporate Movements Confront Globalization*, London: Zed Books.

Sung, Jung Mo, 2002, 'Christian Faith and Globalization', in *Colloquium 2000: Faith Communities and Social Movements Facing Globalization*, ed. Ulrich Duchrow. Studies from the World Alliance of Reformed Churches, 45. Geneva: World Alliance of Reformed Churches, 106–11.

Taylor, Michael, 1990, *Good for the Poor: Christian Ethics and World Development*, London: Mowbray.

— 1995, *Not Angels but Agencies: The Ecumenical Response to Poverty – A Primer*, London: SCM Press.

— 2000, *Poverty and Christianity: Reflections at the Interface between Faith and Experience*, London: SCM Press.

— 2003, *Christianity, Poverty and Wealth: The Findings of 'Project 21'*, London: SPCK.

Tiongco, Romy, 2000a, Is God on the Side of the Poor?, Internal Christian Aid document.

— 2000b, The Reign of God and the Poor, Internal Christian Aid document.

— 2001a, Global Liberalisation and the Poor and Vulnerable, Internal Christian Aid document.

— 2001b, Laws and the Protection of the Vulnerable, Internal Christian Aid document.

— 2001c, Option for the Poor, Internal Christian Aid document.

— 2002, Personal Communication, 19 March.

Trade for Life: Campaign Strategy Paper [2000], London: Christian Aid.

Trigo, Pedro, 1991, *Creation and History*, Maryknoll: Orbis Press.

UK Department for International Development, 2000, *Eliminating World Poverty: Making Globalisation Work for the Poor*, White Paper on International Development. Internet. Available from http://www.dfid.gov.uk/Pubs/files/whitepaper2000.pdf; accessed 22 January 2004.

Urban Rural Mission, 1988, *We Discovered Good News: Brazilian Workers Reread the Bible*, Geneva.

Vásquez, Manuel A., 1998, *The Brazilian Popular Church and the Crisis of Modernity*, with an introduction by Duncan Forrester and Alistair Kee, Cambridge: Cambridge University Press.

Vatican II, 1966, *Pastoral Constitution on the Church in the Modern World: Gaudium et Spes, promulgated by His Holiness Pope Paul VI on December 7, 1965*, Boston: Pauline Books & Media.

Verhelst, Thierry G., 1990, *No Life Without Roots: Culture and Development*, translated by Bob Cumming, London: Zed Books.

Vries, Egbert de, ed., 1966, *Man in Community*, The Church and Society, London: SCM Press.


Wade, Robert, 2001, 'Showdown at the World Bank', *New Left Review* 7:124–37.

White, Sarah and Tiongco, Romy, 1997, *Doing Theology and Development: Meeting the Challenge of Poverty*, Windows on Theology, Edinburgh: Saint Andrews Press.

Wink, Walter, 1984, *Naming the Powers: The Language of Power in the New Testament*, Basingstoke: Marshall Pickering.

— 1986, *Unmasking the Powers: The Invisible Forces That Determine Human Existence*, Minneapolis: Augsburg Fortress.

— 1992, *Engaging the Powers: Discernment and Resistance in a World of Domination*, Minneaplis: Augsburg Fortress.

— 1998, *The Powers That Be: Theology for a New Millennium*, London: Doubleday.

Wolf, Hans-Heinrich, 1971, 'Towards an Ecumenical Consensus', in R. Preston, ed., *Technology and Social Justice*, Valley Forge: Judson Press, pp.425–45.

Wood, Ellen, 1995, *Democracy Against Capitalism: Renewing Historical Materialism*, Cambridge: Cambridge University Press.

World Bank, 2001, *World Development Report 2000/2001: Attacking Poverty*, Washington: World Bank.

— World Development Indicators Database, Washington: World Bank.

World Conference on Church and Society, Geneva, July 12–26, 1966. *Official Report, with a description of the Conference. Christians in the Technical and Social Revolutions of Our Time*, 1967, Geneva: WCC.

World Council of Churches (WCC), 1968, *New Delhi to Uppsala, 1961–1968: Report of the Central Committee to the Fourth Assembly of the World Council of Churches*, Geneva: WCC.

## Online Resources

'Brazil Marks 40th Anniversary of Military Coup: Declassified documents shed light on U.S. role', The National Security Archive at George Washington University, http://www.gwu.edu/~nsarchiv/NSAEBB/NSAEBB118/index. htm; accessed 2 January 2007.

Brazilian Landless Workers Movement Homepage. http://www.mst.org; accessed 2 January 2007.

Centro de Estudos e Ação Social Homepage, http://www.ceas.com.br/; accessed 2 January 2007.

Christian Aid Homepage, http://www.christian-aid.org; accessed 2 January 2007.

Friends of the MST Homepage, http://www.mstbrazil.org; accessed 2 January 2007.

'Harry S. Truman: Inaugural Address, Thursday January 20, 1949', Great Books Online, http://www.bartleby.com/124/pres53.html; accessed 2 January 2007.

International Monetary Fund Homepage, http://www.imf.org; accessed 2 January 2007.

John Lewis Partnership Homepage, http://www.john-lewis-partnership. co.uk; accessed 2 January 2007.

Kwa, Aileen, 2003, 'Power Politics in the WTO', Focus on the Global South, http://www.focusweb.org/publications/Books/power-politics-in-the-WTO.pdf; accessed 2 January 2007.

Miriam-Webster Online Dictionary, http://www.m-w.com; accessed 2 January 2007.

Trade Justice Movement Homepage, http://www.tradejusticemovement. org.uk; accessed 2 January 2007.

UK Department for International Development Homepage, http://www.dfid. gov.uk; accessed 2 January 2007.

'U.S. Department of State Annual Report on International Religious Freedom for 1999: Brazil', Center for Studies on New Religions, http://www. cesnur.org/testi/irf/irf_brazil99.html; accessed 2 January 2007.

'"Vulture fund" investors make millions out of third world debt crisis', Jubilee 2000 Coalition, http://www.jubileeresearch.org/jubilee2000/news/ vulture141000.html; accessed 2 January 2007.

The World Bank Group Homepage, http://www.worldbank.org; accessed 2 January 2007.

World Council of Churches Homepage, http://www.wcc-coe.org; accessed 2 January 2007.

World Trade Organization Homepage, http://www.wto.org; accessed 2 January 2007.

*Fieldwork Diaries*

Much of the discussion in this book comes from fieldwork diaries kept throughout the period from October 1999 to October 2002. The fieldwork diaries were kept every day I worked with CA and CEAS throughout this period in Edinburgh, London, and Salvador Brazil.

There were also 29 interviews with staff and key volunteers, who have each been guaranteed anonymity. The two directly quoted herein are:

*Interview 12*, Glasgow Christian Aid Office, 12/01/00.
*Interview 22*, Edinburgh Christian Aid Office, 25/01/00.

# Index of Names and Subjects